Coal Ash

INNOVATIVE APPLICATIONS OF COAL COMBUSTION PRODUCTS (CCPs)

ACAA

AMERICAN COAL ASH ASSOCIATION

Coal Ash
Innovative Applications of Coal Combustion Products (CCPs)

Editors:
Gregg J. Dienhart
Barry R. Stewart
Samuel S. Tyson

Library of Congress Catalog Card Number: 98-70882

ISBN - 0-9662912-0-4

Copyright © 1998 by the American Coal Ash Association
2760 Eisenhower Avenue, Suite 304
Alexandria, Virginia 22314-4553 USA
Phone: 703-317-2400 FAX: 703-317-2409
Internet- http://www.ACAA-USA.org
E-mail- ACAA-USA@msn.com

Published by the American Coal Ash Association
Printed in the United States of America

Samuel S. Tyson, P.E.

THE AMERICAN COAL ASH ASSOCIATION

The American Coal Ash Association (ACAA) was founded in 1968. ACAA's mission is to advance the management and use of CCPs in ways that are technically sound, commercially competitive and environmentally safe. This mission is accomplished by working with specifiers, designers, contractors, legislators, regulators and others.   ACAA and its members lead in efforts that result in the use of more than twenty-five percent of CCPs each year in the USA. The worldwide use of CCPs exceeds 100 million tons annually.

ACAA serves a worldwide community including producers and marketers of CCPs, coal companies, allied trade groups, consultants, universities and others having commercial, academic, research or related interests in CCPs. ACAA's members have shaped the technical, educational, government relations, communications and marketing programs that allow CCPs to compete effectively with other engineering and manufacturing materials. These programs are primarily funded by membership dues along with fees collected from educational programs and publication sales.

The ACAA Educational Foundation was established in 1995 to create educational opportunities for the advancement of CCP management and use. The Foundation's principal programs have included co-sponsorship with ACAA of international meetings on CCP management and use, the distribution of the resulting technical proceedings to hundreds of universities and an innovative scholarship program. The Foundation has laid solid groundwork for awarding scholarships on a continuing basis to students wishing to pursue an understanding of CCP management and use in conjunction with practically any field of study, and fund-raising activities have been established to perpetuate the Foundation's programs.

ACAA is recognized as the worldwide leader in advancing the beneficial use of CCPs. This reputation has been earned through a wide range of activities including an annual survey and report on CCP production and use; a biannual symposium that attracts registrants from more than thirty countries; an educational program for managers of CCP production and marketing activities; and a membership base that includes all stakeholders in CCP management and use.

This "coal ash book" was assembled through the efforts of ACAA members and others too numerous to mention. In lieu of thanking individual contributors, perhaps a more fitting tribute would be to thank every stakeholder who has helped ACAA to be the organization that is now presenting this valuable document to the CCP industry. Accordingly, this book is dedicated to those who, over many years, not only have had the knowledge and drive to make specific contributions to CCP management and use, but also have had the vision and dedication to magnify and preserve their accomplishments by creating and sustaining ACAA as the standard-bearer for the CCP industry.

Sincerely,

Samuel S. Tyson, P.E.
Executive Director, ACAA
President, ACAA Educational Foundation

INTRODUCTION

Increased energy use and a corresponding increase in the use of coal to generate electricity has resulted in the production of increased quantities of Coal Combustion Products (CCPs). Stringent environmental controls have further increased both the volumes and types of CCPs generated. Coal represents, by far, the largest supply of fossil energy reserves domestically and worldwide. Thus, coal is expected to be a major source of energy far into the next century and CCPs will continue to be produced in substantial volumes.

CCPs are a valuable natural resource; the third largest volume mineral resource produced in the USA (Table 1). Disposing of CCPs puts unnecessary demands on other limited natural resources. CCPs benefit the construction industries by providing cost effective replacements for cement, natural aggregates, fill materials, and other commonly used construction products. Other industries, from agriculture to synthetic zeolites, also benefit from using CCPs.

Most important to the CCP generator is the cost savings of beneficial reuse. In many locations, a CCP management and use program can save significant amounts of money over landfilling or other disposal options. In turn, these factors reduce the cost of electricity to the public, commerce and industry which leads to greater economic growth. Finally, CCP use reduces the volume of solid waste disposed and the volume of natural materials produced, mined or otherwise obtained for construction purposes, benefiting the environment.

The generation of electricity is by far the largest use of coal. Currently, close to a billion tons of coal are burned annually to generate electricity in the USA, and as a result, over 100 million tons of CCPs are produced. With leadership from ACAA over three decades, more than twenty-five million tons of these CCPs are used, and worldwide the use of CCPs exceeds 100 million tons annually.

TABLE OF CONTENTS

AACA'S MISSION IS TO ADVANCE THE MANAGEMENT AND USE OF COAL COMBUSTION PRODUCTS (CCPS) IN WAYS THAT ARE TECHNICALLY SOUND, COMMERCIALLY COMPETITIVE AND ENVIRONMENTALLY SAFE.

Fly ash for filler applications

ACAA and the CCP Industry

The American Coal Ash Association (ACAA) was founded in 1968, eight years before enactment of the federal *Resource Conservation and Recovery Act (RCRA)*, which, as amended, has been the dominant statute governing the management and use of ash derived from the combustion of coal. In the earlier years, ACAA held a unique pioneering status under *RCRA* as a *"resource recovery and recycling"* organization. More recently, ACAA has expanded the scope of its efforts and has worked to establish "product" status for coal ash that is beneficially used. Accordingly, the terminology, coal combustion products (CCPs), is used to include—fly ash, bottom ash, boiler slag, flue gas desulfurization (FGD) material, and other clean-coal combustion materials.

ACAA's mission is to advance the management and use of CCPs in ways that are technically sound, commercially competitive and environmentally safe. ACAA is dedicated to advancing the management and use of CCPs on behalf of the "coal ash industry" worldwide. ACAA works to gain and expand the recognition of CCPs as engineering and manufacturing materials while promoting their use in a variety of markets. ACAA and its members lead in efforts that result in the use of more than twenty-five million tons of CCPs each year in the USA—and worldwide use of CCPs exceeds 100 million tons annually.

CCPs are: produced from the combustion of coal, the principal fuel source for today's electric energy needs; specified by designers and engineers who rely on the availability of CCPs as mineral resources both today and for the twenty-first century; marketed by companies knowledgeable in the use of CCPs as engineering and manufacturing materials; and used in numerous applications throughout the world.

The "CCP industry" is a group of stakeholders connected by common interests in the management and use of CCPs. Worldwide, the CCP industry includes: producers of coal ash, including coal-burning electric generating companies, independent power producers and industrial boiler owners; marketers of CCPs; organizations and individuals, including coal companies, allied trade groups, consultants, universities and others having commercial, academic, research or related interests in CCPs.

The deregulation of the electric power industry, not only in the USA but worldwide, has prompted electric generating companies to evaluate their corporate structure, goals and strategies. The production of low-cost power is essential to their ability to thrive in a highly competitive environment—and CCP management and use is an important part of the overall strategy to reduce costs and generate revenue. ACAA's challenge is to continuously assess the needs of the CCP industry and respond with innovative programs that are both effective and flexible.

Why CCP Management and Use?

The fundamental reasons for having a program dedicated to the management and use of CCPs are to:

- establish and enlarge the recognition of CCPs as engineering and manufacturing materials that compete with other products on the basis of comparable technical, economic and environmental merits;

- promote CCP management practices that maximize recycling quantities, revenue enhancement and environmental safety while minimizing disposal costs and liability;

- develop, compile, maintain and disseminate technical data and reports that increase and support effective uses of CCPs; and

- enhance and support local, state, national and international policies for commerce and the environment by integrating the use of CCPs into sustainable "green" programs to build and rehabilitate the infrastructure.

ACAA's member companies, or "customers," have various needs that are important to the management and use of CCPs. The most fundamental of these needs are to:

- plan and organize a tailored and effective CCP management program;

- identify opportunities for marketing CCPs, both internal to the producing company as well as in external markets;

- create promotional activities for CCP markets;

- maintain existing markets for CCPs;

- pursue new markets for CCPs;

AACA staff members

- control costs of the CCP management program;

- accommodate regulatory, technical and marketing issues affecting CCPs; and

- demonstrate the benefits of CCP management on a continuing basis.

ACAA is the leading trade association, both within the USA and internationally, dedicated to advancing the management and use of CCPs, and membership in ACAA becomes the logical choice for organizations wishing to establish or maintain a CCP management and use program.

Now, more than ever, there is a need in the CCP industry for a trade association that is both proactive and effective in representing shared industry needs. For companies that recognize their need for involvement in and commitment to the CCP industry, the time is right to join with other stakeholders to continually reinvent ACAA and focus its efforts to meet current and future needs.

Goals and Objectives

ACAA provides opportunities for members of the CCP industry to address their needs through joint activities that are both efficient and effective. The goals established to accomplish ACAA's mission are broadly stated in several key areas as follows:

Codes & Standards: Develop consensus standards and guidance documents for the use of CCPs through participation in organizations having both national and international recognition.

Communications: Collect and disseminate information from national and international sources on the management and use of CCPs to ACAA members, materials specifiers, designers, purchasers, project managers, contractors, government agencies, universities and others.

Education: Create understanding and support for the use of CCPs through greater knowledge by educating members of the CCP industry as well as other industry groups, government agencies, legislators, regulators, students and citizen groups.

Government Relations: Coordinate with ACAA members and related industry groups and all levels of government, both within the USA and internationally, to identify issues affecting the management and use of CCPs and to influence related regulations, legislation and guidance documents.

Market Promotion: Identify current and new market conditions and assist members in promoting the many technically sound, commercially competitive and environmentally safe uses of CCPs on par with other engineering and manufacturing products.

Research, Development & Demonstration (R&D): Cooperate with industry groups, government agencies, universities and others to facilitate the creation of needed studies, surveys, databases and instructional programs to advance the management and use of CCPs.

Structure and Governance: Meet the diverse needs of the CCP industry and achieve growth in membership, programs and recognition by maintaining the flexibility to continually develop and refine ACAA's committee and governance structures.

Additionally, various short-term, intermediate and long-term objectives are defined on an annual basis, subject to sound management practices and budgetary constraints. Such objectives are modified from time to time as priorities change and as new needs are identified.

Benefits of Membership

Membership in ACAA provides support for the development, implementation and maintenance of effective programs for the management and use of CCPs. There are numerous benefits resulting from the use of CCPs—the most fundamental being the avoidance of disposal costs by CCP producers, and the creation of revenue streams by both producers and marketers. ACAA members report significant benefits from CCP management and use programs, including CCP promotional activities, pursued in conjunction with ACAA membership. Such benefits are based on a variety of factors such as the amount and type of CCP produced, local market conditions and other variables. The benefits from membership and participation in ACAA's programs and activities are briefly described as follows—

Unified Industry Voice
- manage CCPs as a mineral resource to conserve natural resources
- market CCPs as engineering and manufacturing materials
- represent CCP industry in national standards committees and industry groups
- provide information to government, industry and public sectors worldwide

Table 1

LEADING MINERAL

RESOURCES PRODUCED

IN THE USA

(Similar information is available for other countries.)

Mineral Resources	Annual Production (million short tons)
Crushed Stone	1,350
Sand & Gravel	980
CCPs	100
Portland Cement	90
Iron Ore	65

[Sources: United States Department of the Interior, *Mineral Commodity Summaries; and,* American Coal Association, *CCP Production & Use Report.*]

- coordinate activities to address liability issues
- assist in the development of sound engineering practices
- serve as a centralized source of technical information
- create and present educational programs

Information Exchange and Networking
- meet with specifiers, purchasers and users of CCPs
- produce technical papers for publication and presentation
- develop consensus standards and guides for the use of CCPs
- identify regulatory and legislative opportunities
- participate in trade shows and exhibitions
- distribute promotional items and literature
- provide networking opportunities

Educational Opportunities and Professional Growth
- hold regular committee meetings and educational workshops
- host international symposia on management and use of CCPs
- publish workshop and conference proceedings
- provide educational programs for CCP managers
- distribute newsletters, technical brochures and general information
- produce technical papers, reports, manuals and videos
- create technical assistance programs tailored to industry needs
- facilitate exchanges of technical information

Market Awareness and Development
- coordinate the implementation of consensus standards for use of CCPs
- expand government policies for procurement of CCPs
- compare CCPs to competing materials and products
- reduce CO_2 emissions from other industries through increased use of CCPs
- advance the use of CCPs as technically sound, commercially competitive and environmentally safe products
- remove technical, legal and regulatory barriers to CCP use
- support "infrastructure development" and "sustainable growth" using CCPs
- distribute published materials for educational and promotional activities

Educational Meetings

ACAA sponsors educational meetings in the form of one-day workshops on topics related to CCP management and use. ACAA also offers a one-week educational program, the CCP Managers Program. The program is tailored for CCP producers, marketers and related industry representatives and continuing

education credits are issued through a university co-sponsor. ACAA's International Symposium on Management and Use of CCPs is held in January of odd-numbered years. Proceedings volumes are published through a cooperative agreement with the Electric Power Research Institute (EPRI). The author of each paper makes a presentation during sessions arranged throughout the week-long event. ACAA's symposia have attracted authors and attendees from some forty countries over the years. ACAA has enhanced the symposium by developing agreements among international participants to encourage the open and free exchange of technical information.

Publications

Ash at Work, ACAA's newsletter, plus technical and executive memoranda, communicate information to ACAA's members and others about ACAA programs, meetings, staff activities, publications and events related to the management and use of CCPs.

ACAA's annual report on Production and Use of CCPs contains detailed information on CCPs used in numerous applications. The report is updated annually and is used by government agencies and industry groups. Producers and marketers of CCPs also use the information as a tool for planning and evaluating CCP management programs. Technical papers in ACAA's library provide information on CCP production and use throughout the world.

ACAA's library contains more than 1200 entries. Topics include: technical papers and reports, manuals, white papers, compilations of papers on selected topics, annotated slide sets and videos. Full sets of proceedings volumes currently are available from ACAA's international symposia from 1987 to the present, and individual papers are available from 1967.

The use of volcanic ash in the Roman Colosseum has allowed it to endure for centuries. This basic structural "glue", in the form of coal fly ash, has been used in recent decades for modern sports arenas such as: Jacobs Field in Cleveland; the Marine Midland Center in Buffalo; Turner Field in Atlanta; and the Jack Kent Cooke Stadium (pictured) near the District of Columbia.

This coal-fired electric power plant is located only three miles from the U.S. Capitol. The plant, for many years in an undeveloped setting, is now a good neighbor in its residential setting.

FLY ASH PARTICLES ARE SPHERICAL IN SHAPE IN CONTRAST TO PORTLAND CEMENT PARTICLES WHICH ARE ANGULAR.

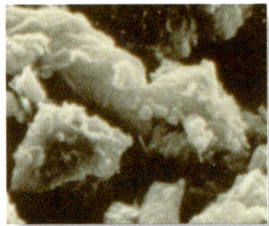

Fly Ash

Bottom Ash

Boiler Slag

FGD Material

CCPs include fly ash, bottom ash, boiler slag and flue gas desulfurization (FGD) material and other clean coal combustion products.

Cenospheres, a small but important percentage of CCPs, are processed to meet desired particle size and density requirements. These hollow spherical particles have many applications in the filler industry.

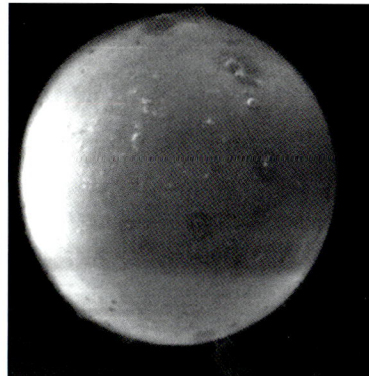

TYPICAL SPHERES OF TWO DIFFERENT SIZES

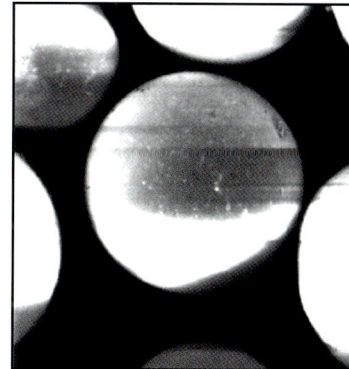

75 μm

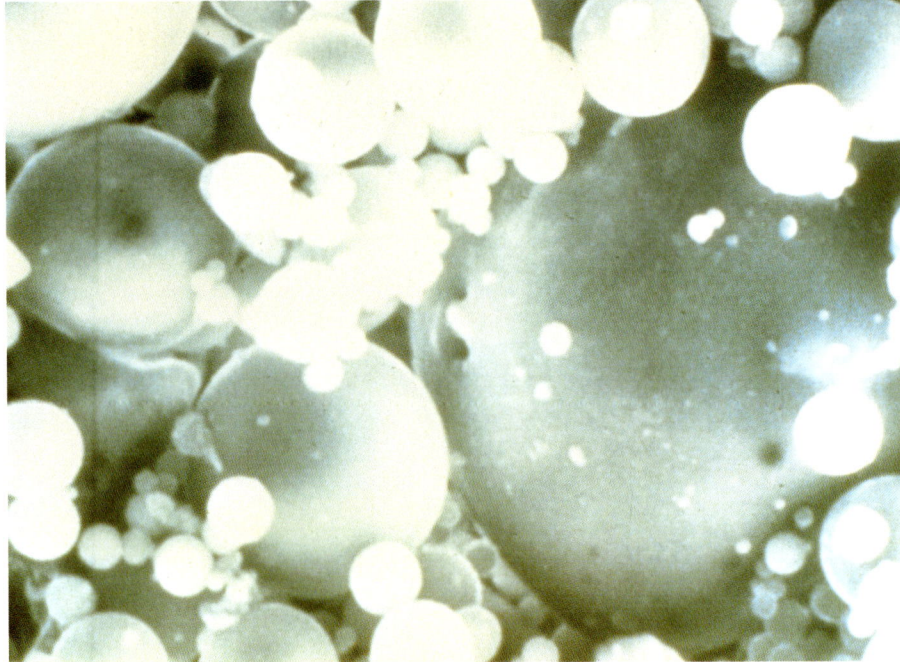

The spherical nature of fly ash particles can easily be observed when magnified 2000 times.

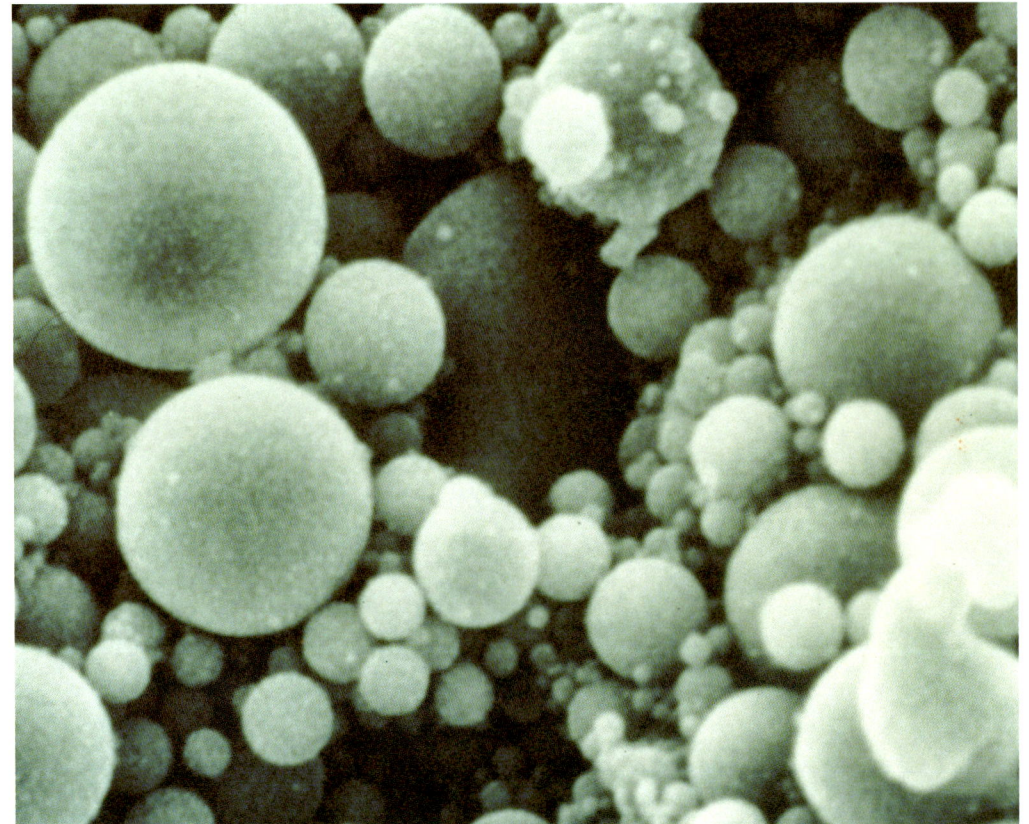

The spherical shape of fly ash is important in many applications.

Fly ash has a powdery appearance and fine texture. It feels very much like talcum powder to the touch.

Boiler slag feels like coarse sand.

CONCRETE PRODUCT
APPLICATIONS

Fly ash is a vital component
in the high-strength concrete
that made possible the
magnificent structures that
grace the Chicago skyline.

CORETTE LIBRARY CARROLL COLLEGE

Concrete containing fly ash is produced
at a central batching plant and then
distributed to job sites by trucks.

Fly ash is handled and
transported much like cement, in
pneumatic tanker trucks.

Fly ash concrete was used in the decking and piers of the cable-stayed Sunshine Skyway bridge across Tampa Bay in Florida.

In Virginia, fly ash concrete was used in the decks and piers of this highway bridge.

Fly ash concrete culvert and spillway.

A large quantity of fly ash was incorporated into the arched spans and piers of this concrete bridge in the District of Columbia.

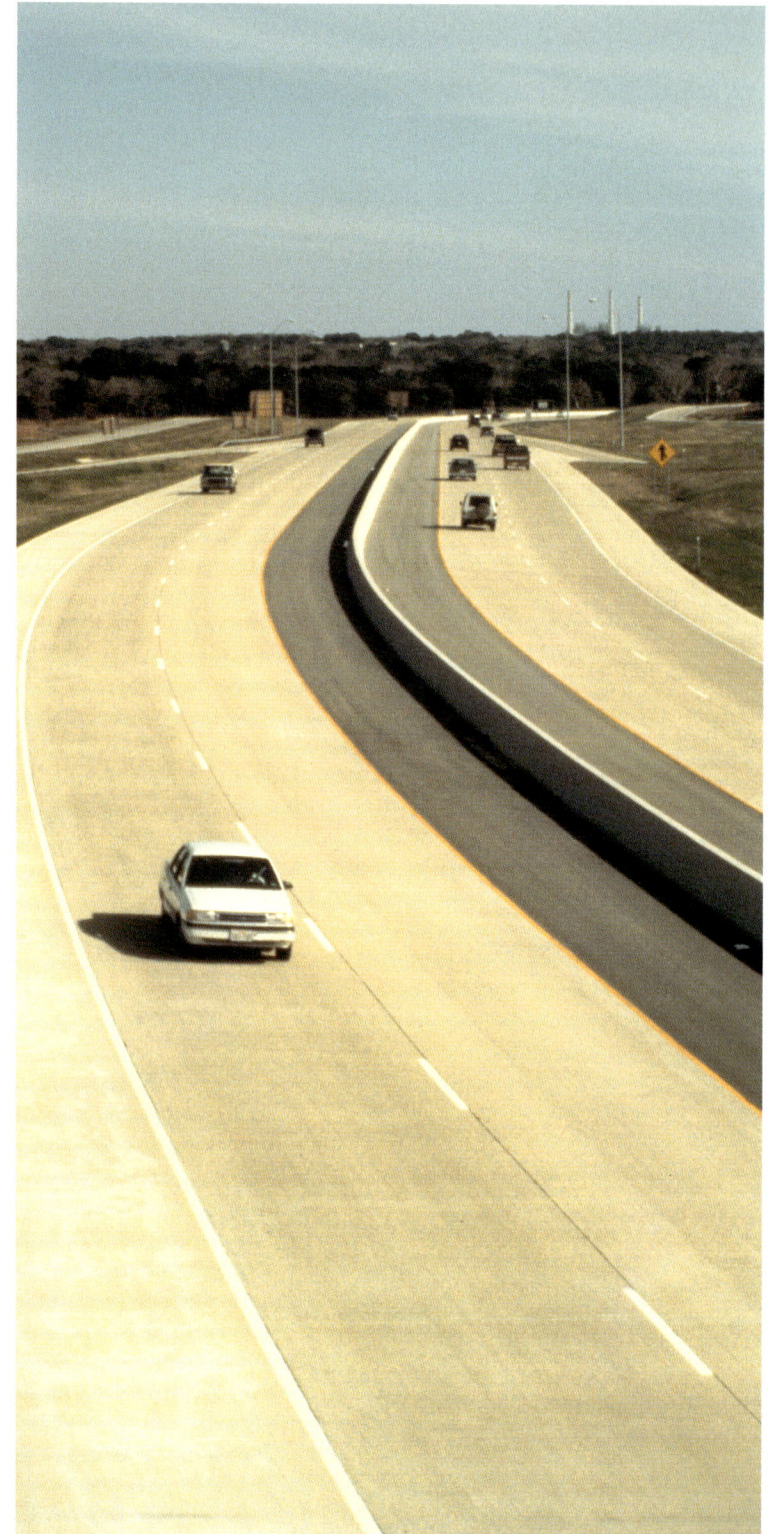

Concrete pavement containing fly ash is very durable and cost effective.

Fly ash is an important component in mass concrete projects such as this dam. Fly ash lowers the heat of hydration, which reduces the likelihood of cracking and also contributes to a long-term strength gain.

Fly ash is an important component in interstate pavements across the USA.

Architectural exposed concrete is both durable and esthetically pleasing, in this case, after nearly twenty years.

Boiler slag was used as an exposed aggregate in precast and in cast-in-place concrete for this building.

The fly ash concrete frame of a building in progress.

Concrete parking lots and cart paths made with fly ash provide durability and complement the idyllic setting of this award-winning golf course.

The strength and durability characteristics of fly ash concrete are ideal for a variety of structures like this embassy and underground parking garage complex.

The combined qualities of strength and appearance of concrete using fly ash and mineral pigment, allow its use both in the structure and in the facade.

Massive slabs of fly ash concrete supported tower cranes on the grounds of the U.S. Capitol building during bicentennial renovations.

High-strength fly ash concrete enables this building to stand atop intersecting lines of a subway transfer station.

Miami, Florida

24

A fly ash concrete structure is the foundation and retaining wall supporting the engraved panels of the Vietnam Veterans Memorial in the District of Columbia.

CCPs removed from a disposal site were used in lieu of imported soil to construct this roadway embankment. Environmental benefits included the preservation of virgin materials and the extended life of the disposal site.

Following construction of the CCP embankment, a fly ash concrete pavement was installed.

Compacted fly ash for structural fill beneath a highway access ramp.

A combination of fly ash, lime, and portland cement was used to stabilize this pavement base during airport construction.

Fly ash, lime, and cement were used extensively in base stabilization in the construction of runways and aprons for the Newark, New Jersey Airport.

In Texas, the Houston International Airport used fly ash and lime for base stabilization.

A combination of lime treatment and fly ash used to stabilize clayey base material.

Self-cementing (high calcium) fly ash used for in-place stabilization of pavement base layers.

Fly ash stabilized base material used in the construction of rural roads.

For larger highway projects, fly ash stabilized base material may be distributed from a central mixing plant.

Fly ash used as a stabilizing agent for full-depth pavement recycling.

Asphaltic pavements containing bottom ash and fly ash.

Common Geotechnical Applications

CCPs with optimum moisture content are transported by conventional means for dust-free use: water treatment facility (top); roadway (lower left); and parking area (lower right).

Flowable Fill Applications

Flowable fill typically contains fly ash and water and may contain small amounts of portland cement. Filler materials such as bottom ash and sand are commonly added. Optimum flow characteristics are provided by the spherical fly ash particles with a minimum amount of water.

The technical and economic advantages of flowable fill have been achieved on a variety of projects including: massive backfills (top) with significant savings in avoided labor and equipment costs; bridge replacements (lower left) with major savings over new construction costs; and fills between roadway and bridge structures where future maintenance costs are avoided due to the thoroughness with which even the most inaccessible voids are filled.

Flowable fill can be mixed in a
pugmill and delivered efficiently by
conventional ready mixed concrete trucks.

Flowable fill serves as the foundation for the Marine Midland Arena in Buffalo, New York.

Flowable fill performs well in situations where access for ordinary compaction equipment is restricted.

Flowable fill is ideal for filling utility trench cuts quickly and safely with a minimum of effort, even in busy traffic conditions.

Flowable fill and precast concrete culverts speed construction and dramatically cut costs on rural bridge replacement projects. In the sequence below, a deteriorated bridge span (top) is replaced by first installing concrete culverts under the span to carry stream flow (middle) and finally placing flowable fill to cover the culverts and encase the old structure.

An approach to a major river crossing is formed with large volumes of flowable fill poured from a nearby roadway without the need for direct access to the site.

This office park was constructed on a fly ash structural fill.

Real estate development can be facilitated on a variety of sites using CCP materials as structural fill.

LARGE VOLUME CCP
STRUCTURAL FILLS FOR
SITE PREPARATION

30,000 tons for warehouse expansion.

30,000 tons for church parking lot.

250,000 tons for school sports complex.

Dallas, Texas

Fly ash was used as a replacement for a portion of the portland cement in these concrete barriers.

Bricks made from clay and fly ash.

The gypsum produced by wet scrubbers is used in the manufacture of high quality wallboard.

This CCP derived aggregate is as easy to handle, store, market and distribute as conventional aggregates.

A high quality aggregate manufactured by sintering pelletized fly ash.

THESE MARBLE-SIZED AGGREGATES ARE STRONG, LOW-DENSITY AND ARE SUPERIOR TO NATURAL AGGREGATES FOR LIGHTWEIGHT STRUCTURAL CONCRETE AND MASONRY UNITS.

CCP aggregates manufactured, processed and stockpiled for future delivery.

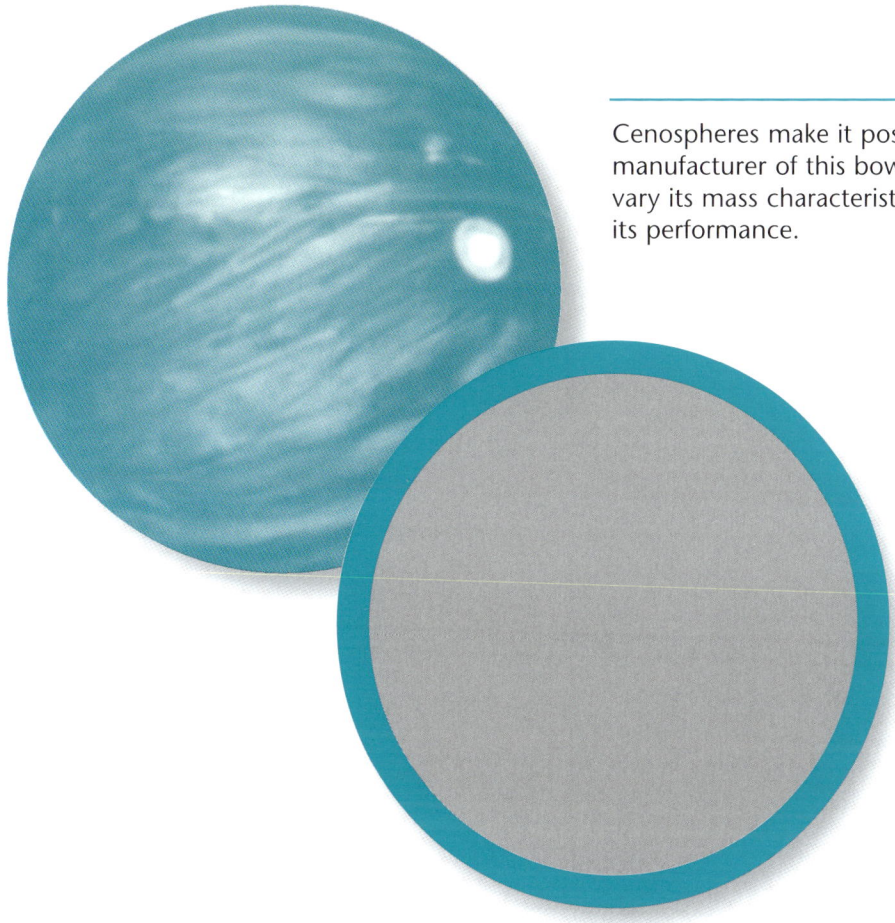

Cenospheres make it possible for the manufacturer of this bowling ball to vary its mass characteristics and tailor its performance.

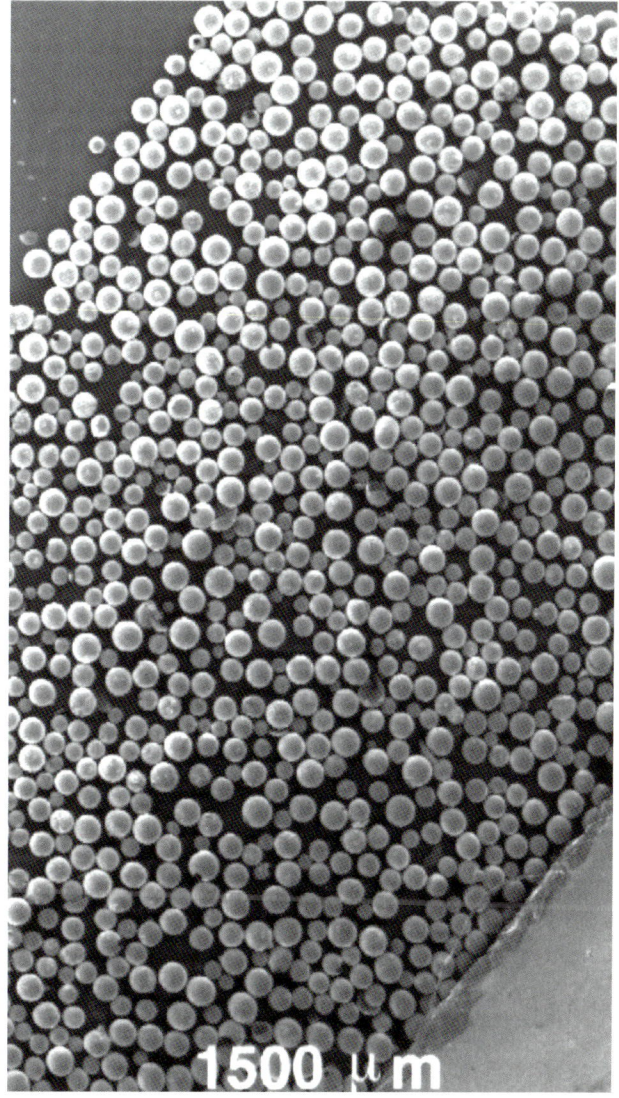

Cenospheres are processed to meet specific size requirements (right) and can be supplied throughout a range of available sizes (bottom).

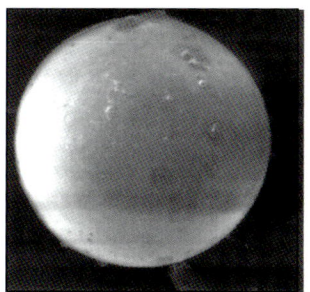

75 μm

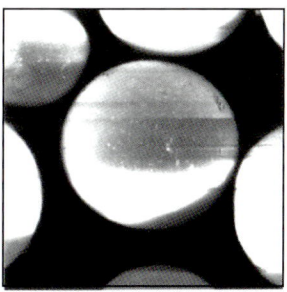

1500 μm

The buoyancy of cenospheres, or "floaters", causes them to rise to the surface of CCP ponds where they are retrieved for use.

Cenospheres as well as denser fly ash particles are used as filler in paints.

Precast concrete panels containing fly ash are stockpiled awaiting shipment.

Autoclaved cellular concrete may contain up to 70% fly ash. These blocks are widely used in construction in Europe and their use is growing in U.S. markets.

CCPs support sustainable development and "green building" standards: structural fill for site preparation; brick and concrete block; gypsum wallboard; asphalt shingles; paint and plastic products; concrete and asphalt driveways.

FLY ASH IS USED AS
MINERAL FILLER IN THE
BACKING MATERIAL FOR
ROOFING SHINGLES WHILE
BOTTOM ASH AND BOILER
SLAG ARE USED AS
GRANULES ON THE
SHINGLE SURFACE.

Incorporating fly ash in the manufacture of polyvinyl chloride (PVC) pipe improves productivity and lowers the raw material costs. Automobile manufactures also incorporate fly ash in the production of plastic parts.

These blocks contain both bottom ash and fly ash. Bottom ash was used as aggregate, while fly ash was used to replace a portion of the portland cement.

Salt Lake City, Utah

CCPs improve the chemical and physical characteristics of soils, promoting plant growth and increasing productivity.

Fly ash was added to soil on the right side of photograph, increasing water infiltration and retention, allowing a drought-prone soil to become more productive.

FGD material was applied to this field with a fertilizer spreader, providing calcium, sulfur and trace minerals for enhanced plant growth. This CCP application resulted in a healthy stand of forage.

A spinner spreader can be used both to apply FGD gypsum to replace agricultural gypsum or to apply high calcium CCPs to replace agricultural limestone.

CCPs used to convert a muddy quagmire to a clean, dry cattle lot.

This durable dry pad for use in hay storage is made of compacted CCPs

CCP Land Reclamation Project Nurtures New Growth

During the construction of an airport, the land on this site was stripped of its topsoil leaving a barren wasteland. The lack of plant cover led to severe erosion. CCPs were applied increasing water infiltration and retention. The site now supports a vigorous stand of vegetation and the erosion has been arrested.

The use of fly ash to replace cement in concrete has the potential to eliminate 10 to 14 million tons of CO_2 annually. This and other green building techniques using CCPs support sustainable growth.

Atlanta, Georgia

Volunteers plant trees at a CCP storage facility in support of the environmental commitment by the CCP industry to a sustainable future.

CCPs are incorporated into coal refuse to amend poor growing conditions. The improvements resulting from this CCP application will assure successful revegetation.

Poor site conditions due to low water retention, acidic materials and nutrient imbalances (left side) have been ameliorated by the incorporation of CCPs (right side).

Many of the impediments to reclamation are removed by CCPs. This test plot was treated with CCPs and supports lush vegetation, in contrast with the surrounding untreated material.

This hillside was denuded by emissions from a smelting operation (left). CCPs were part of a successful reclamation plan to restore vegetative growth.

The ACAA Educational Foundation creates opportunities to advance the knowledge of CCP management and use through its programs which include: an international symposium co-sponsored with ACAA; a one-week university curriculum for CCP managers; the distribution of technical materials to hundreds of university students in practically all fields of study; and scholarships awarded for academic excellence related to the management and use of CCPs.

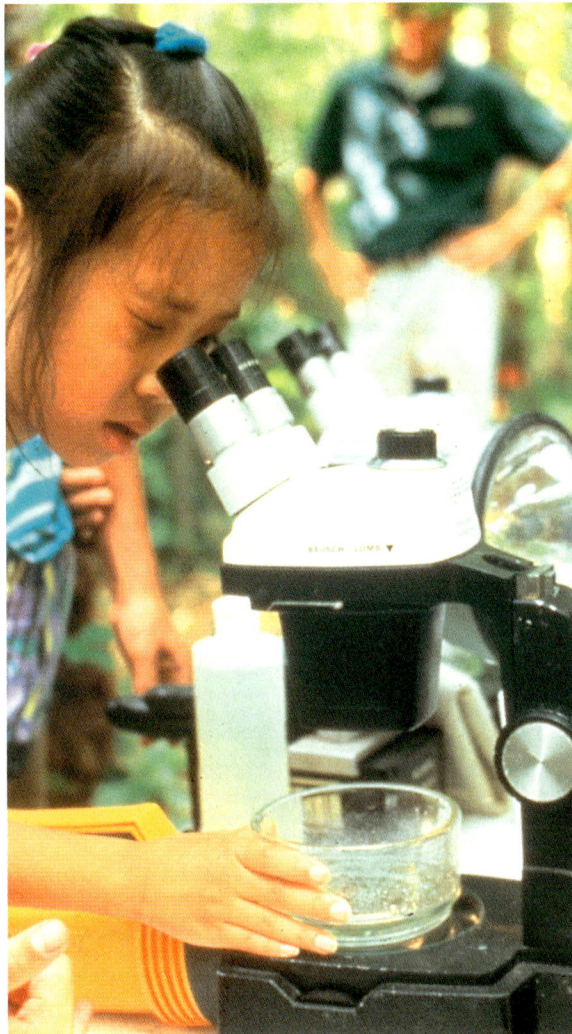

ACAA member companies support educational programs for students to promote environmental awareness.

Environmental stewardship relies on a recognition of all things, great and small. Founded in 1968 in the USA, ACAA is now the worldwide leader in advancing the management and use of CCPs in harmony with technical, commercial and environmental policies and goals.

INTERNATIONAL PROJECTS

Fly ash has been used for more than fifty years in concrete projects around the world. More than nine million metric tons of fly ash are used each year throughout Europe for concrete applications including dams, power stations, offshore platforms, tunnels, highways, airports, commercial and residential buildings, bridges, pipelines and silos.

The dam of Permantokoski hydro power plant was constructed in the early 1960s with concrete containing fly ash. The dam is located in the north of FINLAND.

The East bridge, linking the Islands of Funen and Zeland, in **Denmark**, will be the world's largest suspension bridge. It is made with high-performance concrete containing fly ash. The structure has an expected life of 100 years.

The European Association for Use of the By-Products of Coal-Fired Power Stations (ECOBA) has membership from some fifteen countries and shares ACAA's basic goals for advancing the management and use of CCPs. In support of such goals, ACAA and ECOBA have cooperated in a successful exchange of information since 1993.

The Castor and Pollux towers in Frankfurt, **Germany** utilize high-strength concrete containing fly ash. The massive foundation also used fly ash for strength as well as to control heat of hydration.

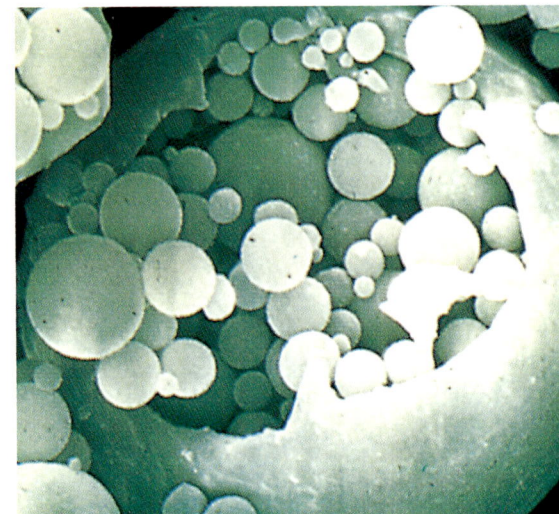

Photomicrograph of spherical fly ash particles.

Fly ash concrete was used in the construction of the Picasso tower in Madrid, **Spain**. Pumpability of the concrete was a major design consideration and fly ash was a key component in the mixtures.

The Caixa Geral Depositos Bank in Lisbon, **Portugal** was constructed in 1994 using concrete with fly ash. This important fifteen story building was designed to accommodate 3,600 employees.

The Puylaurent dam, completed in 1995, is one of the largest arch dams built in **France** in the past decade. The use of fly ash in concrete controlled the heat of hydration during hardening and decreased the risk of cracking due to thermal stress.

Fly ash concrete was mixed on-site for renewal of a landing strip of the Eindhoven Airport in **The Netherlands**. The concrete was placed in a single layer.

A railway tunnel was built in Vienna, **Austria** during the 1980s. The fly ash concrete for this underground structure is impermeable to water and resistant to sulfate attack.

A precast concrete pole, designed to carry overhead electric lines, was manufactured with fly ash and lightweight aggregate in **Italy** to improve environmental durability and significantly reduce the weight of the pole.

The B.P. Harding Gravity Base Structure was built to store up to 570,000 barrels of crude oil. The structure was towed 540 nautical miles from **England** and submerged in over 300 feet of water in the North Sea. The marine environment demanded an extremely durable concrete while other design parameters required high-strength lightweight characteristics which were provided by a sintered fly ash lightweight aggregate.

Several concrete mixes incorporating fly ash were used in the construction of the Torness Power Station, a nuclear electricity generating plant in **Scotland**. Fly ash concretes with high percentages of fly ash were used for their impermeability, pumpability, reduction of thermal strain and associated cracking, sulfate resistance and long-term strength gain.

Designed for a 100-year service life, The Channel Tunnel provides a fast rail link between **England** and **France**. This engineering feat relied on the use of quality fly ash for concrete and grouts.

The Genk-Langerlo power generating station in **Belgium** has concrete storage towers for fly ash. The use of fly ash in this concrete resulted in smooth and even surfaces.

Fly Ash

Bottom Ash

Boiler Slag

FGD Material

Table of Contents

CCPs compete for a share of practically every engineering and manufacturing market in which minerals are used. As depicted in the figures to the right, the leading CCP applications in the USA are: concrete; road base; snow and ice control; structural fill; waste stabilization; blasting grit and roofing granules; and a myriad of other applications. In this section, the numerous CCP applications that were shown in the preceding pictorial sections are briefly described along with the variety of other important CCP applications.

LEADING FLY ASH USES

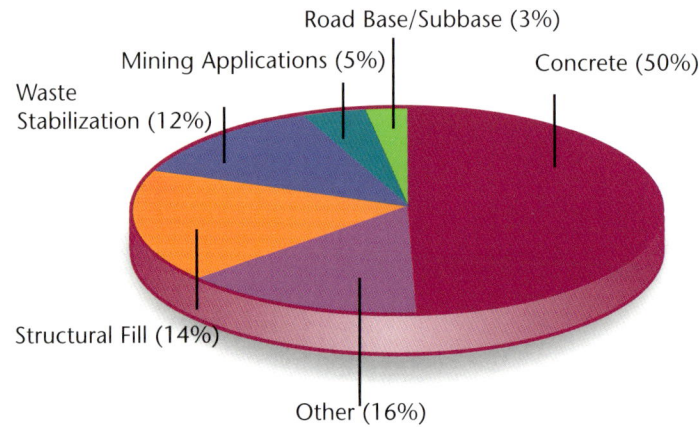

Road Base/Subbase (3%)
Mining Applications (5%)
Concrete (50%)
Waste Stabilization (12%)
Structural Fill (14%)
Other (16%)

LEADING BOTTOM ASH USES

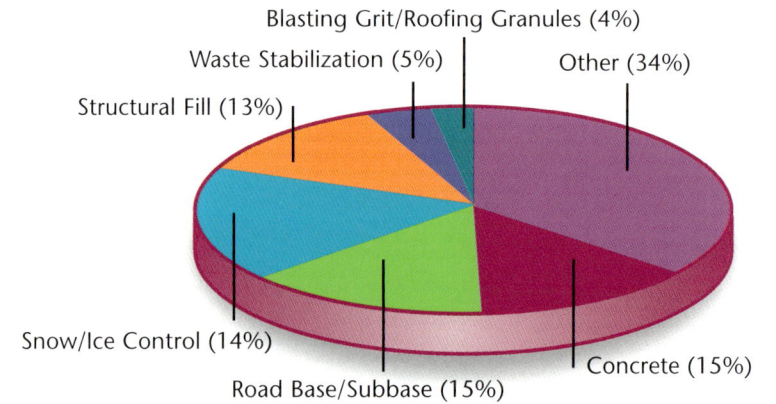

Blasting Grit/Roofing Granules (4%)
Waste Stabilization (5%)
Other (34%)
Structural Fill (13%)
Snow/Ice Control (14%)
Road Base/Subbase (15%)
Concrete (15%)

LEADING BOILER SLAG USES

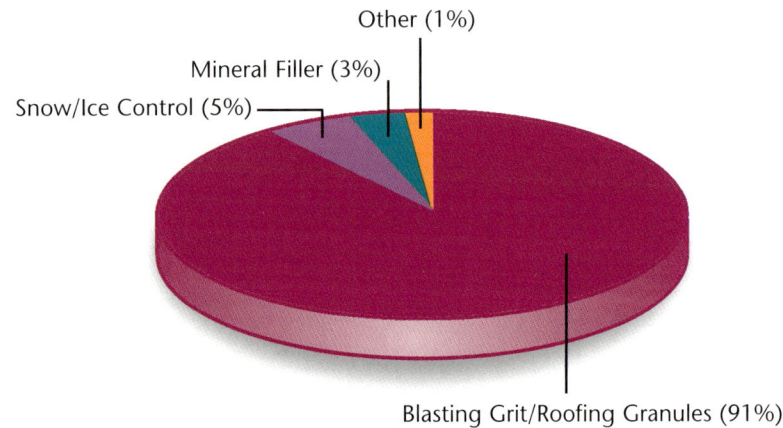

Other (1%)
Mineral Filler (3%)
Snow/Ice Control (5%)
Blasting Grit/Roofing Granules (91%)

LEADING FGD USES

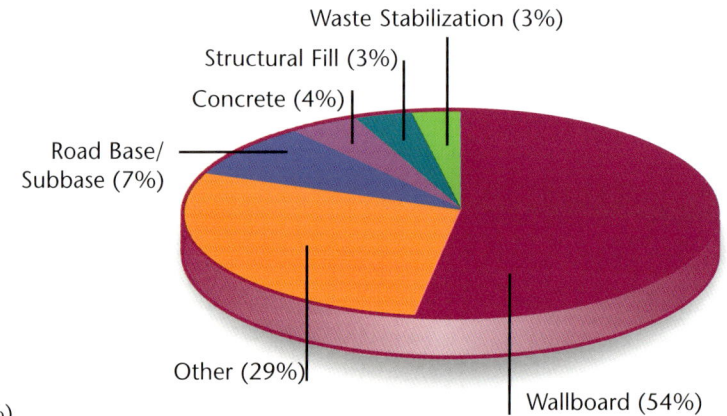

Waste Stabilization (3%)
Structural Fill (3%)
Concrete (4%)
Road Base/Subbase (7%)
Other (29%)
Wallboard (54%)

TYPICAL CCP USE
by Type

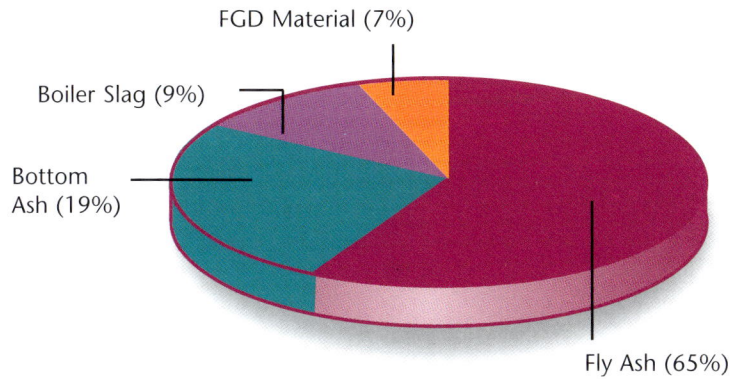

FGD Material (7%)

Boiler Slag (9%)

Bottom Ash (19%)

Fly Ash (65%)

*Typical use figures for each type of CCP.
Percentages vary from year to year.*

CCP USE
by Year

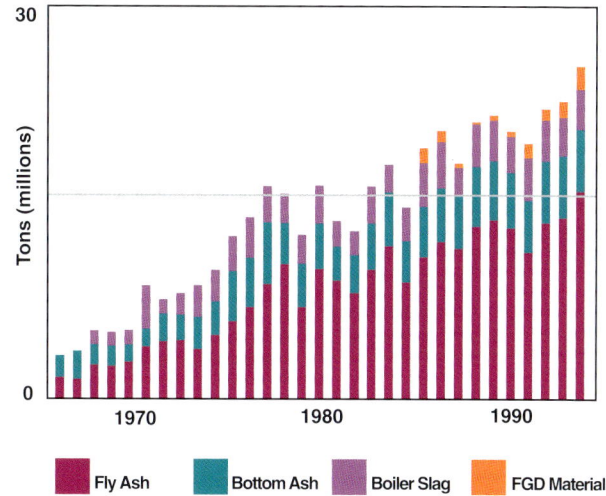

Tons (millions)

30

0

1970   1980   1990

■ Fly Ash   ■ Bottom Ash   ■ Boiler Slag   ■ FGD Material

TYPICAL CCP PRODUCTION
by Type

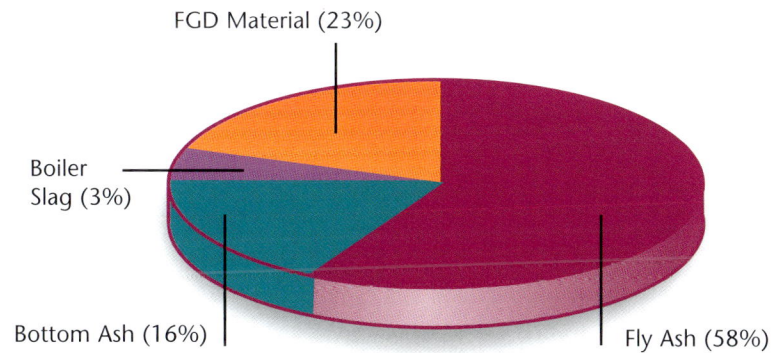

FGD Material (23%)

Boiler Slag (3%)

Bottom Ash (16%)

Fly Ash (58%)

*Typical production figures for each type of CCP.
Percentages vary from year to year.*

CCP PRODUCTION
by Year

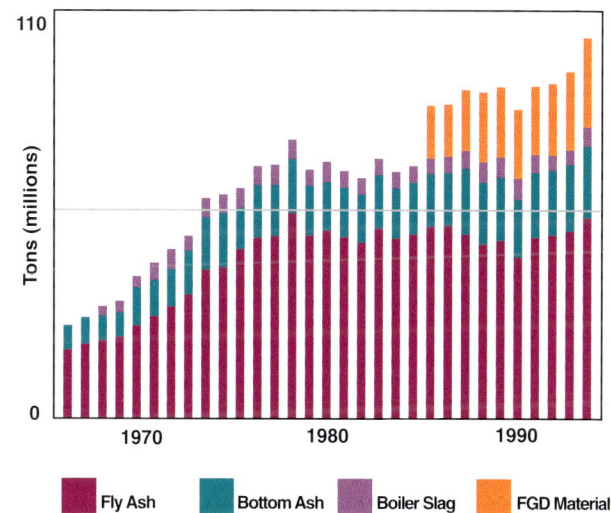

Tons (millions)

110

0

1970   1980   1990

■ Fly Ash   ■ Bottom Ash   ■ Boiler Slag   ■ FGD Material

The American Coal Ash Association (ACAA) has compiled data on the production and use of coal combustion products (CCPs) for more than thirty years. The quantities of CCPs produced during that period have steadily increased beyond 100 million tons annually while the quantities of CCPs used have increased at an even faster rate.

In the USA, CCPs have become the third most abundant mineral resource, ranking below crushed stone and sand & gravel, and above portland cement and iron ore. The annual percentage of CCPs that are used has grown to approximately thirty percent of production in the USA. Worldwide, more that 100 million tons of CCPs are used each year.

CCPs are produced and used in every state in the USA. Electricity accounts for about one-third of primary energy use in the United States. More than half of this electricity is produced by coal-fired electric utilities where the total annual consumption of coal is around one billion tons. Along with the production of electric power, generating stations in the USA produce more that 100 million tons of coal combustion products (CCPs) each year.

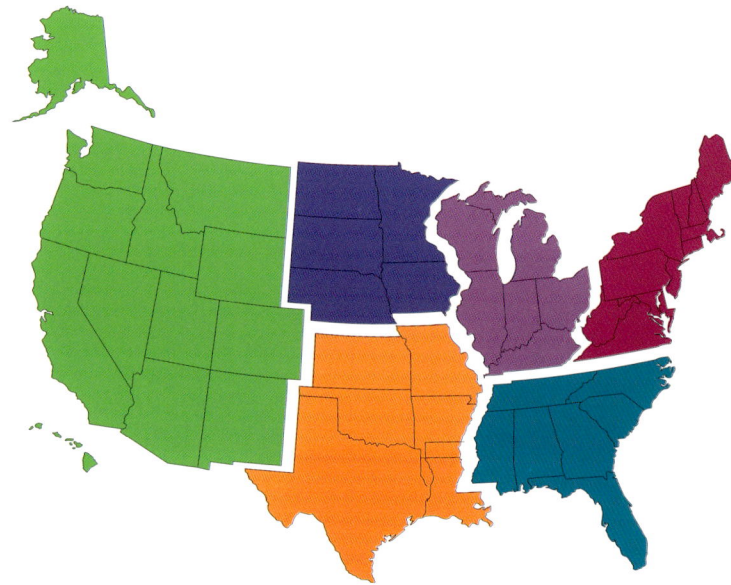

Region I   Region II   Region III
Region IV   Region V   Region VI

TOTAL CCP PRODUCTION
by Type and Region

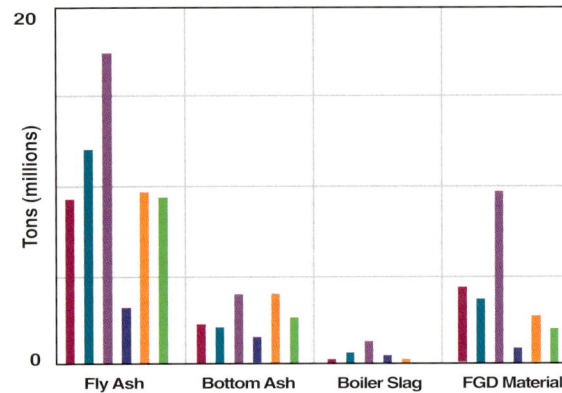

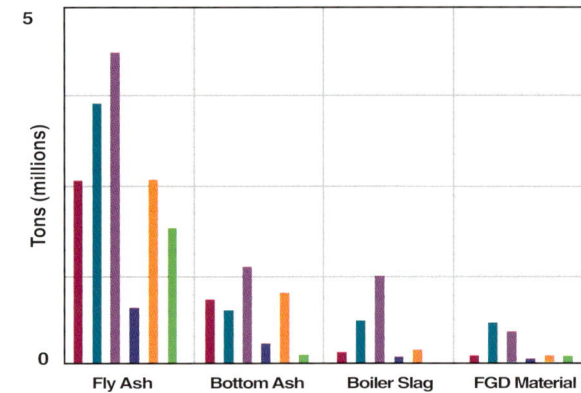

TOTAL CCP USE
by Type and Region

Introduction

Increasing energy demands for the foreseeable future will continue to be met by burning coal. Today in the USA, over sixty percent of energy needs are supplied by the combustion of coal and coal will continue to supply a majority of the energy consumed well into the twenty-first century. The USA has over 225 billion tons of proven coal reserves, enough to last over 200 years at current usage rates. Coal can be used to generate electricity cleanly, due to advancements in technology. Emissions of sulfur dioxide (SO_2) and nitrous oxides (NOx) have been greatly reduced over the past thirty years, and advancements continue to occur which will further reduce admissions and protect the environment. In meeting world energy requirements, even greater amounts of CCPs will be produced.

The relative concentrations of the various chemical compounds found in CCPs vary considerably. Factors affecting the concentrations of the various chemical compounds are coal type and source, coal preparation processes, boiler design and combustion conditions, CCP collection and handling methods and the characteristics of any additives. Thus, while the general nature of a given source of CCPs will be known, specific characteristics will vary from source to source as well as over time from a single source. This situation is analogous to changes in other common engineering and manufacturing materials such as sand and gravel and portland cement, which also vary from source to source and over time at a given source.

Coal Types

The characteristics of CCPs depend greatly upon the type of coal from which they are produced. The four basic types of coal are anthracite, bituminous, subbituminous and lignite. Additionally, some energy plants burn either culm and gob, mining wastes from coal-cleaning activities.

Anthracite, sometimes known as hard coal, has a heating value above 13,500 Btu/pound. It is commonly used as metallurgical coal, although some anthracite is used for power production. The volume of CCPs produced from the combustion of anthracite coal, by comparison to other types of coal, is small, and the calcium oxide (CaO) content of the ash is relatively low. Bituminous coal has a heating value between 10,500 and

14,000 Btu/pound and may be classified by sulfur and ash contents that range from high to low depending on the specific region from which it is mined. The CCPs from bituminous coals generally are low in CaO. Subbituminous coal, sometimes known as soft coal, has a heating value between 8,300 and 11,500 Btu/pound and may be classified by sulfur content which can be quite low, relative to other coal types. The volume of CCPs from subbituminous coal can range from high to low, and the CaO content is generally higher, by a factor of two or more, than that of CCPs from other types of coal. Lignite coal, commonly referred to as brown coal, has a heating value between 6,300 and 8,300 Btu/pound, produces a relatively high volume of CCPs that can be either high or low in CaO content depending upon the region of origin. The mining wastes, culm and gob, are high in ash content (45% to 70%), and low in heating value (2,500 to 6,500 Btu/pound). If used for producing energy, most culm and gob are burned in fluidized bed combustion (FBC) boilers. Typically, power plants of this type are located near mine sites or coal-cleaning waste piles.

Coal-Fired Combustion Boilers

Coal ash is produced in electric power plants by the burning of coal in steam boiler furnaces. The furnace is equipped for continuous combustion and the coal is injected or conveyed into the furnace where combustion takes place. The coal ash, or non-combustible portion of the coal, is collected from the bottom of the boiler or exits the boiler in the flue gas stream to be captured using dust collection devices.

There are several different manufactures of coal combustion steam boiler furnaces, each with different design features. However, the basic types of boilers can be grouped into the following categories:

- pulverized dry-bottom boiler;
- pulverized wet-bottom boiler;
- cyclone boiler;
- stoker-fired boiler; and
- fluidized bed combustion (FBC) boiler.

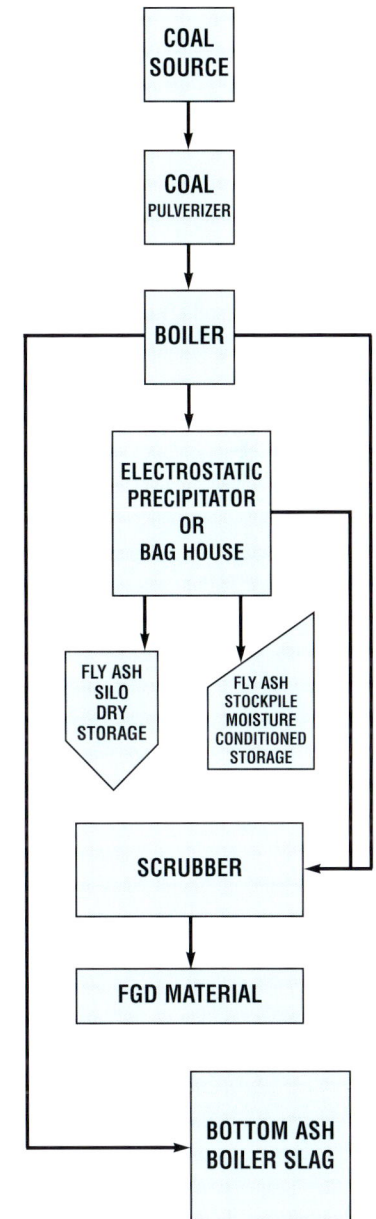

A typical flow of materials through a pulverized coal boiler system.

Common Uses of Fly Ash

Raw material in portland cement manufacture

Replacement for cement in concrete and grout

Cement replacement in precast concrete products

Ingredient in aerated concrete

Mineral filler in asphaltic concrete

Aggregate for the stabilization of highway subgrades

Aggregate for road base material

Raw material for manufacture of lightweight aggregates

Material for structural fill

Material for flowable fill

Raw material for metal reclamation

Filler material in plastics, paints and metals

Sanitary landfill cover or liner

Backfill for controlling subsidence in abandoned mines

Backfill for fighting mine fires

Soil amendment

Raw material in brick manufacture

Ingredient in the manufacture of roofing felt

Raw material for making mineral wool insulation

Acidic mine drainage control

Material for absorbing oil spills

Medium for filtering insulating oil used by utilities

Absorbent for dewatering sewage sludge

Fixation ingredient for sulfate sludge

Flowability agent in molding sand

Material for plant growth media

Pulverized coal boilers make up the majority of the coal fired boilers used by electric utilities. With pulverized coal boilers, the coal is pulverized to a fine powder (70% < 75 (µm) and injected into the boiler with preheated air for combustion. In a pulverized dry-bottom furnace, the ash particles are formed in suspension and approximately eighty percent of the coal ash, known as fly ash, remains entrained in the flue gas and exits the furnace, where it is collected by mechanical collectors, electrostatic precipitators or baghouses. The remaining approximately twenty percent of the coal ash is removed from the bottom of the furnace and is known as dry bottom ash, sand sized particles with granular characteristics.

In a slag-tap furnace, or pulverized wet-bottom boiler, up to fifty percent of the ash forms on the walls of the boiler. The molten ash falls into a tank of water at the bottom of the furnace where it is quenched into a hard, black and glassy material known as boiler slag. The other fifty percent of the coal ash exits the furnace with the flue gas as fly ash.

The cyclone boiler is capable of burning a wide variety of fuels. Coals burned in cyclone boilers need to be crushed but do not need to be pulverized. Due to this larger particle size, the cyclone furnace retains seventy to eighty percent of the coal ash as slag that is removed from a slag tank located beneath the furnace. The remainder of the coal ash exiting the cyclone furnace as fly ash, entrained in the flue gas, and is captured by dust collectors.

Stoker-fired boilers were one of the earliest types of boilers used for the combustion of coal in energy production. The coal is sized to a two-inches or smaller and fed into the boiler using a chain grate or other conveying device. The coal is retained in the boiler on the conveying device until combustion of the coal is complete. Because the coal in a stoker is not pulverized, the combustion is not as efficient compared to other boiler types. Therefore, the ash typically has a high unburned carbon content, usually greater than ten percent and as high as sixty percent. The fly ash and bottom ash are formed and removed from the boiler in the same manner as a pulverized coal boiler. Because of the sizing of the coal, the fly ash is typically coarser than fly ash from other boilers. Fly ash is typically eighty percent of the coal ash produced by a stoker boiler, with the remainder being bottom ash.

Fluidized bed combustion (FBC) boilers are being used in increasing numbers for the combustion of coal due to stricter emission standards. FBC boilers can be used to burn high-sulfur fuels with efficiency while maintaining the low levels of SO_2 air emissions required by regulatory agencies. Typically with FBC boilers, coal is sized to one-half inch or less and injected into the boiler with limestone or some other form of calcium carbonate. The calcium reacts with the sulfur in the boiler and prevents the formation of SO_2 gas. Compounds of sulfur and calcium, typically calcium oxide (CaO), calcium sulfate ($CaSO_4$), calcium sulfite ($CaSO_3$), and calcium hydroxide ($Ca(OH)_2$), are produced in addition to coal ash. The finer particles, FBC fly ash, are removed from the flue gas stream by a baghouse or electrostatic precipitator and the coarser, heavier particles, known as FBC bed ash are removed at the bottom of the boiler.

FBC boilers are also used to combust fuels with low heating values such as culm and gob. These fuels have BTU values as low as 2500 Btu/pound and have ash contents of as high as seventy percent. Because of the combustion chamber design and fuel handling capabilities of an FBC boiler, these fuels can be burned efficiently with low emission levels for the production of power.

Other coal combustion technologies such as Integrated Gasification Combined Cycle (IGCC) and Pressurized Fluid Bed Combustion (PFBC) are emerging from the U.S. Department of Energy's Clean Coal Technology Program into commercialization. The ashes and slags from these boilers have considerably different characteristics than the CCPs from the aforementioned conventional boiler types. These coal combustion technologies will play a major role in power production in the twenty-first century.

At any given power plant, the design and operation of the boilers and the characteristics of the coal that is burned will determine the amounts of fly ash, bottom ash, and boiler slag that is produced.

For relative comparison, consider a typical 500 megawatt coal-fired power plant which is assumed to burn 1.5 million tons of coal annually. If the coal contains ten percent ash, the plant would produce 150,000 tons of CCPs. If the plant utilized any one of the three common furnace types as shown below, CCPs would be produced in differing proportions in each case as follows:

- Dry-bottom furnace—30,000 tons of bottom ash and 120,000 tons of fly ash;

- Wet-bottom furnace—75,000 tons of boiler sag and 75,000 tons of fly ash; and

- Cyclone furnace—105,000 tons of boiler slag and 45,000 tons of fly ash.

If the sulfur content of the coal warranted the use of wet scrubbers for SO_2 control at the power station, the plant would generate up to another 250,000 dry tons per year of flue gas desulfurization (FGD) material.

Clean Coal Technology

Coal is the world's most plentiful fuel, accounting for over 94 percent of the proven fossil energy reserves in the U.S., with similar situations existing in both developed and developing countries. The U.S. Department of Energy (DOE) and the private sector have been engaged in an eight-billion dollar clean coal technology (CCT) program since the mid-1980s, with an overall goal of bringing about environmental improvements in the use of coal for the generation of electric power. The total funding of the CCT program has come primarily from private sector commitments.

The new coal combustion technologies developed by the CCT program also produce new and interesting CCPs with tremendous potential for use as engineering and manufacturing materials. One such CCP, Limestone Injection Multistage Burner (LIMB) material, results from the injection of dry limestone sorbent into a boiler at a point above the burners. The sorbent then travels through the boiler, capturing SO_2, and is removed with the fly ash. Another such CCP, spray dryer material, is produced when a lime slurry is sprayed into a flue gas stream still containing fly ash. Each of these CCPs are described in the following section

on emission control systems and in a subsequent section on characteristics of CCPs in a table where the typical elemental analysis of both spray dryer material and lime injection material are shown.

Emission Control Systems

CCPs are removed from the flue gas stream using one or a combination of the following: electrostatic precipitators; fabric filters; mechanical collectors; and FGD systems.

Electrostatic precipitators are available in a broad range of sizes for utility and industrial applications. Collection efficiency can be expected to be 99.8% or greater of inlet dust loading. Electrostatic precipitators work by electrically charging the ash particles in the flue gas to collect and remove them. The units comprised of a series of parallel plates through which the flue gas passes. The negatively charged particles are attracted toward the grounded collection plates where they accumulate. The ash layer is removed by "rapping" which consists of a sudden striking of the plates. The particles fall into collection hoppers directly below the collection plates.

Fabric filters, commonly known as baghouses, collect the dry particulate matter as the cooled flue gas passes through the filter material. As the particulate accumulates on the bags, the pressure drop increases across the filter and the bags must be cleaned. Cleaning is done by reversing the air flow through the filter. The ash cake dislodged during cleaning falls into a hopper directly below the bags and is removed by an ash transfer system. Collection efficiency can be expected to be at least 99.8%. Baghouses have the potential for enhancing SO_2 capture in installations downstream.

Common Uses of Bottom Ash

Raw material in portland cement manufacture

Aggregate in flowable fill

Aggregate in cold mixed asphalt

Ingredient in bituminous stabilized bases for highways

Aggregate in cement stabilized bases for highways

Abrasive grit for snow and ice-covered roads

Filter material

Structural fill

Common Uses of Boiler Slag

Sand blasting grit

Filter medium for water treatment

Raw material for mineral wool insulation

Roofing granules in asphalt shingles

Grit for ice-covered roads

Structural fill and road bases

Aggregate in highway construction

Common Uses of Flue Gas Desulfurization (FGD) Material

Raw material in portland cement manufacture

Flowable fill

Structural fill

Mining applications

Wallboard manufacture

Soil Amendment

Mechanical dust collectors, often called cyclones, have been used extensively to separate large particles from flue gas streams. The cyclonic flow of gas within the collector creates centrifugal force on the ash particulate which drives the ash particles out of the flue gas stream. Hoppers below the cyclones collect the particulate and feed an ash removal system. The mechanical collector is most effective on particles larger than ten microns. For smaller particles, the collection efficiency drops considerably below ninety percent. Mechanical collectors are no longer used as primary control devices.

FGD emission control systems may be added to one of the aforementioned types of boilers, particularly pulverized, stoker, and cyclone boilers. FGD systems incorporate the injection of calcium products (lime or limestone) or other sorbents (e.g., sodium, magnesium oxide, ammonia) into the flue gas stream for the removal of sulfur dioxide (SO_2). The basic types of FGD systems are wet scrubbers, spray dryers, and limestone or lime injection.

In wet FGD systems, the fly ash is usually removed from the flue gas stream prior to the flue gas entering the scrubber. In the scrubber, a water/lime slurry is sprayed into the flue gas stream and the SO_2 is removed by the precipitation of calcium sulfate or calcium sulfite. Within the loop, a surge tank is used to control slurry flows and a thickener is used to remove solids.

In spray drying, lime is added to water to produce a slurry. The slurry is sprayed as a fine mist into the flue gas, which still contains the fly ash particulate. The mist reacts with SO_2 and passes to a baghouse or electrostatic precipitator where both the FGD residue and fly ash are collected dry without separation.

In direct injection systems, lime or limestone is injected into the boiler for SO_2 control. In each of these FGD control systems, lime particles chemically combine with SO_2 and oxygen to form calcium sulfate ($CaSO_4$), unreacted lime (CaO), and calcium sulfite ($CaSO_3$). The calcium and sulfur compounds along with the fly ash are removed from the fllue gas by a baghouse or electrostatic precipitator.

CCP Handling and Storage

The most common method of conveying fly ash is pneumatic conveyance of the dry material. Fly ash is dry when collected in precipitators and bag houses. Due to its fine particle size, it is easily conveyed and stored in a dry condition. For applications such as cement admixture, the material can be shipped in bulk pneumatic tankers and stored in silos similar to other dry, fine materials like flour and portland cement.

For applications such as structural fills where the ash is to be handled like soil or aggregate, about twenty percent moisture is added to the fly ash. This process is called "conditioning". The conditioning process may be performed using a pugmill, rotating drum, or other form of bulk material mixer as the ash is loaded from silos to truck.

Fly ash is frequently conveyed to storage ponds near power plants with large quantities of water. Utilization of ash sluiced to ponds requires drainage and drying prior to use for most applications.

High CaO fly ash from subbituminous and lignite coal is most commonly handled dry to avoid the hardening reactions that typically occur on contact with water.

Bottom ash and boiler slag are most commonly handled wet and conveyed to storage areas by sluicing. The coarse grain size of the materials allows for relatively easy drainage in ponds or in bins. These materials are commonly handled in a damp or moist condition for utilization.

FGD material from wet scrubbers typically must be dewatered before use or disposal; however, in some cases it is sluiced and stored in ponds. Dry FGD materials are conditioned with water to facilitate handling, utilization, and disposal.

Characteristics of CCPs

CCPs are composed largely of oxides of silicon, aluminum, iron, and calcium, together with smaller quantities of magnesium, titanium, potassium, phosphorus, sulfur, and alkali compounds. These compounds are present in the coal or are added during coal processing.

CCPs from pulverized boilers, cyclone boilers, and stoker fired boilers are produced in three forms:

- **fly ash** is a fine grained material transported out of the boiler by the flue gas and collected in a baghouse or precipitator;

- **bottom ash** is a coarse grained material which is collected at the bottom of either a pulverized or stoker fired boiler, and

- **boiler slag** is a coarse grained material which is collected in a water-filled tank beneath a cyclone fired boiler.

CCPs are solid, inert materials. A microscopic view of fly ash particles shows that it is a spherical, fused material, similar in size to portland cement and lime (right). An elemental analysis of bituminous coal fly ash shows that it is similar to clay soils found in the eastern USA (Table 1). Both coal fly ash and clay soils are primarily composed of oxides of silicon, aluminum, and iron; and both contain trace amounts of other oxides.

TABLE 1

Typical Elemental Analysis of Conventional Coal Fly Ash & Common Clay Soil

Compound	Coal Fly Ash	Clay Soil
SiO_2	46%	42%
Al_2O_3	26%	28%
Fe_2O_3	17%	17%
CaO	3.8%	2.8%
SO_3	2.6%	2.6%
K_2O	1.5%	1.6%
TiO_2	1.1%	1.4%
MgO	1.1%	0.9%
Na_2O	0.6%	1.6%
P_2O_5	0.3%	2.1%

A portion of fly ash is hollow, gas-filled, glassy microspheres called cenospheres. Cenospheres are formed when CO_2 and N_2 fill the semi-molten material in the coal-fired boiler. Cenospheres are usually less than one percent of the total mass of CCPs produced. They are generally gray to buff in color and are composed primarily of silica and alumina. They resemble fine sand in grain size and will float to the surface of ash ponds where they are gathered by skimming. They can be very valuable as fillers for use in the manufacture of paints, plastics, ceramics, adhesives, and metal alloys. The low density of cenospheres also provides excellent insulating properties.

Electron micrographs of fly ash (left) and portland cement (right).

Hotel and Parking Garage

Other types of CCPs are generated by fluidized bed boilers, wet FGD scrubbers, spray dryers, and limestone or lime injection boilers. The CCPs generated from these units primarily consist of calcium oxide (CaO) calcium sulfate ($CaSO_4$), calcium sulfite ($CaSO_3$), and calcium hydroxide ($Ca(OH)_2$), and, depending upon the system design, these materials may be mixed with fly ash. Typical wet scrubber material contains a mixture of these materials: $CaSO_3 \cdot CaSO_4 \cdot \frac{1}{2} H_2O$, $CASO_3 \cdot \frac{1}{2} H_2O$, $CaSO_4 \cdot 2 H_2O$ and $CaCO_3$. Tables 2 and 3 provide the typical chemical characteristics for other types of these CCPs.

As the prevalence of these types of units increases in the future, a corresponding increase in these products will result. The projected increase in CCP production is and will continue to be generated by environmental control systems.

TABLE 2

Elemental Analysis of Spray Drier and Lime Injection materials

Major Elements	Spray Drier Material	Lime Injection Material
Al	9.0%	10.6%
Ca	22.6%	29.0%
Fe	2.9%	7.7%
K	0.6%	0.9%
Mg	0.4%	0.4%
S	5.4%	2.0%
Si	13.1%	7.9%

TABLE 3

Elemental Analysis of FBC Fly Ash and Bed Ash

Major Elements	FBC Fly Ash	FBC Bed Ash
Al	4.4%	2.1%
Ca	33.1%	45.0%
Fe	4.6%	4.3%
Mg	1.2%	1.2%
P	0.1%	0.1%
S	2.2%	1.4%
Si	10.3%	5.1%

Due to variations in coal, sorbents, combustion equipment and collection devices, the data contained in Tables 2 and 3 may not be representative of materials collected from similar systems.

Specifications and Guidelines for the Use of CCPs

The American Society for Testing and Materials (ASTM), the American Association of State Highway and Transportation Officials (AASHTO), and others have developed a variety of standards for the use of CCPs in many applications.

Use-Specific ASTM Standards

There are numerous ASTM standards which specify CCP characteristics for specific manufacturing and engineering uses. While the following list is by no means all-inclusive, typical ASTM standards that are widely recognized by designers, specifiers and regulators are as follows:

- **ASTM C 311** Standard test methods for sampling and testing fly ash or natural pozzolans for use as a mineral admixture in portland cement concrete;

- **ASTM C 593** Standard specification for fly ash and other pozzolans for use with lime;

- **ASTM C 595** Standard specification for blended hydraulic cements;

- **ASTM C 618** Standard specification for coal fly ash and raw or calcined natural pozzolans for use as a mineral admixture in concrete;

- **ASTM D 5239** Standard practice for characterizing fly ash for use in soil stabilization;

- **ASTM D 5759** Standard guide for characterization of coal fly ash and clean coal combustion ash for potential uses; and

- **ASTM E 1861** Standard guide for use of CCPs in structural fills.

Fly ash for use in portland cement concrete represents the largest usage for CCPs. The applicable standard is ASTM C618, or the very similar standard AASHTO M 295. Each standard characterizes fly ash as either Class F or Class C. Class F fly ash is normally formed from burning bituminous or anthracite coals. Class F fly ash is a pozzolan and will combine with lime or portland cement to form cementitious compounds, but typically is not self-hardening with the addition of only water. Class F fly ash is normally gray in color. Class C fly ash results from burning subbituminous or lignite coals. Most Class C fly ash is alkaline, self-hardening and will form cementitious compounds when moisture is added. Class C fly ash is often brown or tan in color. The American Concrete Institute (ACI) has several technical committees and related reports addressing the use of fly ash in concrete.

The grain size of CCPs is normally determined using the standard procedures of ASTM D 422 or AASHTO T 88. The procedures of ASTM D 554 or AASHTO T 100 are commonly used to determine coal ash specific gravity.

The specific gravity of fly ash ranges from 2.1 to 2.9; boiler slag and bottom ash specific gravity normally ranges from 2.3 to 3.0.

Compacted fly ash and bottom ash usually have dry densities in the range of 70 to 110 pounds per cubic foot. Standard test procedures ASTM D 698 and D 1557 and AASHTO T 99 and T180 are commonly used to define the compaction behavior of CCPs.

Standards for other applications of CCPs have been developed by other groups. For example, fly ash for use in oil well filling is specified by the American Petroleum Institute in its Specification Number 10.

One of the first large-volume use of CCPs was by the U.S. Army Corps of Engineers in construction of the Hungry Horse Dam in the late 1940s. The Corps and the U.S. Bureau of Reclamation have since built several dams using coal fly ash and continue to perform research on its use. The Corps' specifications for military and civil construction projects provide for fly ash use in concrete as well as in subgrade stabilization, embankments, flowable fill, soil amendment, and asphalt filler.

Federal Aviation Administration has created standards which provide for fly ash use in concrete for pavements including airport runways and related facilities.

Typical Tests for CCP Quality and Acceptance

Chemical	*Elemental Analysis (Majors in Ash)*
	Leachate Analysis
	pH
	Loss on Ignition
	Flash Point
	Oil and Grease Solids
	% Volatile Solids
	Corrosivity
Physical	*Gradation*
	Fineness
	Specific Gravity
	Moisture Content
	Particle Shape and Texture
Engineering	*Compaction*
	Shear Strength
	Compressibility
	Permeability
	Pozzolanic Activity
	Age Hardening
	Bulk Density
	California Bearing Ratio (CBR)
Variations in Ash Produced	*Within a Unit*
	Between Units
Variations with Exposure	*Dry Storage/Stockpile*
	Wet Storage/Pond

Cenospheres

Regulations and Guidance for the Use of CCPs

Support for the use of CCPs from government agencies is based on the recognition of technical, economic, and environmental benefits. CCPs that are recycled for useful purposes constitute a major volume of material that would otherwise be disposed. The use of CCPs conserves natural resources and avoids the energy consumption and related emissions associated with the mining and processing natural materials. Additionally, the use of CCPs saves landfill space, creates jobs, revenue and can reduce construction costs.

Federal Regulation

The principal federal statute under which hazardous and solid wastes are regulated is the Resource Conservation and Recovery Act (RCRA) of 1976, as amended. RCRA establishes a comprehensive cradle to grave system for regulating hazardous wastes. Specifically, Subtitle C of RCRA and its implementing regulations impose requirements on the generation, transportation, storage, treatment and disposal of hazardous wastes. To trigger these requirements, a material must be a "solid waste" and the solid waste must be "hazardous". Subtitle D of RCRA pertains to State or Regional Solid Waste Plans. Wastes which are not considered hazardous under Subtitle C fall under Subtitle D and are subject to regulation by the states as solid waste.

As originally drafted, RCRA did not specifically address whether CCPs fell under Subtitle C as a hazardous waste or Subtitle D as a solid waste. In 1980, Congress enacted the Solid Waste Disposal Act amendments to RCRA. Under the amendments, certain wastes, including CCPs, were excluded from Subtitle C regulation. This regulatory exemption is commonly referred to as the "Bevill Amendment."

The amendments further directed that the U.S. Environmental Protection Agency (EPA) produce a report regarding CCPs and recommend appropriate regulation. In 1988, EPA issued its report to Congress, (Wastes from the Combustion of Coal by Electric Utility Power Plants). The EPA report concluded that CCPs do not exhibit hazardous characteristics and that regulation of CCPs should be under Subtitle D.

In 1993, EPA issued its final regulatory determination on the large volume wastes from the coal-fired electric utilities. This ruling continues to exempt fly ash, bottom ash, boiler slag and FGD materials from regulation as hazardous wastes. EPA concluded that "fly ash, bottom ash, boiler slag, and FGD material generated from coal-fired utilities pose minimal risks to human health and the environment."

Federal Guidance for Use of CCPs

The federal government has promoted CCP use through a variety of initiatives. In 1983, EPA promulgated the first federal procurement guideline that required agencies using federal funds to implement a preference program favoring the purchase of cement and concrete containing fly ash. EPA has published a summary of information pertaining to CCP use in an "environmental fact sheet," Guideline for Purchasing Cement and Concrete Containing Fly Ash [EPA/530-SW-91-086, January 1992]. The EPA also endorses the use of pozzolans, such as coal ash, as the preferred method for stabilizing certain metal-bearing wastes.

Most recently, Executive Order 12873, Federal Acquisition, Recycling and Waste Prevention, directs federal agencies to develop affirmative procurement programs for environmentally preferable products. A federal Comprehensive Procurement Guideline (CPG) designates products containing recovered materials, including CCPs.

The CPG designates twenty-four recycled-content products for which government procuring agencies need to develop affirmative procurement programs. These guidelines require all federal agencies and all state and local government agencies and contractors that use federal funds to implement a preference program favoring the purchase of such environmentally preferable products. Through the use of these guidelines, the federal government intends both to expand its use of products with recovered materials, and to help develop markets for them in other sectors of the economy.

State Environmental Regulations

Most states currently do not have specific regulations addressing all uses of CCPs and requests for CCP uses are handled on a case-by-case basis or under generic state recycling laws or regulations. States without formal CCP use regulations or guidelines often encourage the use of coal fly ash in cement and concrete applications and products. Additionally, state highway departments are required by the Federal Highway Administration (FHWA) to have specifications conforming to federal procurement guidelines for cement and concrete containing coal fly ash for federally funded projects.

Several states have adopted laws and regulations or issued policies and/or guidance regarding CCP use; however, the CCP uses authorized from state to state may vary widely. Some states authorize liberal use of CCPs, while others authorize CCP use only in limited applications. In addition, the level of regulatory control and oversight varies significantly.

ACAA periodically publishes a report, State Solid Waste Regulations Governing the Use of CCPs. The information in this report provides an overview of state solid waste laws, regulations, policies and agency guidance governing the use of CCPs. This report is useful to ACAA members and others who are familiar with "beneficial use" regulations for CCPs in their particular state and assists in the exchange of regulatory guidance to enhance the use of CCPs.

Environmental Aspects of CCPs

Large quantities of CCPs have been used in numerous utilization projects over several decades. This history of successful use has demonstrated the environmental acceptability of CCPs.

In addition to conserving natural resources, saving landfill space and generating revenue and jobs, the increased use of fly ash in concrete offers a meaningful contribution to the reduction of carbon dioxide (CO_2), a greenhouse gas associated with global warming. The use of coal fly ash in concrete displaces some of the portland cement, thereby reducing the amounts of fossil fuel and calcined limestone needed for the manufacture of portland cement. Consequently, the potential for reduced emissions of CO_2 from the cement industry through the use of fly ash in concrete ranges from 10 to 14 million tons of CO_2 annually.

The decades of experience and successful utilization projects have fostered commercial and governmental acceptance and knowledge of the use of CCPs as construction and manufacturing materials. While the principal use of fly ash has been in concrete, substantial amounts have also been used in structural fills, soil

stabilization, asphalt mixes and cement manufacturing. Bottom ash has been used as pavement base, pipe bedding, skid control, and in block manufacturing. Boiler slag applications include sand blasting grits, roofing granules, skid control and as a raw material in cement manufacturing. More recently, FBC materials and FGD materials have been used in structural fills, pavement base and backfills. FGD gypsum has been used as a direct replacement for mined gypsum in the production of wallboard and as an additive in cement manufacture.

Concrete Product Applications

The largest volume use of CCPs is in cement and concrete applications. Fly ash is used as a mineral admixture for ready mixed concrete and in the manufacture of cements, aggregates, blocks, precast pipes, panels and autoclaved cellular concrete. Bottom ash is used in cement-treated base and subbase and as an aggregate for concrete block. Boiler slag is used as filler in the manufacture of asphalt for flexible pavement systems.

Mineral Admixture in Concrete

Coal fly ash, like cement and volcanic ash, is composed of oxide compounds found in limestone, iron ore, silica sand and clay. More than 8 million short tons (7.3 million metric tons) of coal fly ash are used annually in cement and concrete products throughout the United States. The amount of fly ash in typical structural concrete applications is in a range from 15 to 35 percent, by weight of total cementitious material, with amounts up to 70 percent in massive walls, girders, and dams. Coal fly ash is available in virtually every location in the United States, including Hawaii and Puerto Rico. Fly ash also is traded internationally.

Early users of coal ash included the U.S. Bureau of Reclamation, the U.S. Army Corps of Engineers and the Tennessee Valley Authority. Their interest in fly ash was based on its pozzolanic properties. The Bureau of Reclamation's experiences with pozzolans in general dates back to the period between 1911 and 1916, when cement for Arrowstock, Lahontan, and Elephant Butte dams was prepared at the damsites, with the first major use of coal fly ash in concrete being the repair of a tunnel spillway at the Hoover Dam in 1942. The Hungry Horse Dam,

Architectural Concrete

Mass Concrete Dam

near Glacier National Park in Montana, was constructed during the period 1948-52 with concrete containing coal fly ash, as were the Canyon Ferry Dam (1954), Palisades Dam (1958), and Yellowtail Dam (1966). Between 1940 and 1973, the Bureau used fly ash in more than 7,000,000 cubic yards of concrete. The Bureau continues to specify coal fly ash, and has used it in countless concrete pipe projects.

Between 1957 and 1959, the Corps used fly ash in 611,000 cubic yards of concrete in the Sutton Dam on the Elk River in West Virginia. This project was part of the Corps' Civil Works program, which now allows fly ash in concrete whenever it is economically available. The Corps' Military Works Program has used fly ash concrete in numerous projects since the 1950s.

The Tennessee Valley Authority (TVA) began using fly ash as a partial replacement for portland cement in the mid 1950s. TVA's first use of fly ash in concrete dates back to 1956 at the Johnsonville Steam Plant, after which fly ash was used in all major construction projects. TVA used 10,600 tons of fly ash from its Gallatin Steam Plant in 94,000 cubic yards of concrete placed at the Normandy Dam in 1976. TVA also used fly ash in the construction of its Watts Bar Nuclear Plant.

The addition of coal fly ash produces concrete with improved strength, durability and placement properties including greater long-term strength gain, improved sulfate resistance, lower heat of hydration, lower permeability, lower water demand, reduced bleed water, increased resistance to alkali-silica reactivity and improved workability.

Fly ash produces beneficial hardened concrete properties through pozzolanic reactions as the concrete cures. ASTM C 618 is a specification standard covering the use of fly ash as a concrete additive when cementitious or pozzolanic properties are desired. The use of this standard assures that fly ash used as a concrete admixture conforms to a specified range of physical and chemical properties. Conformity assures that a consistent, high quality product is produced.

Fly ash can be added during the concrete batching process or directly to the cement. When added in the concrete batching process, fly ash is added along with portland cement, sand, gravel and water to the specific proportions determined in the concrete mix design.

Cement Manufacturing

Fly ash, bottom ash and boiler slag have all been used as raw materials in the manufacture of cement. Coal ash is used because it contains silica, alumina, calcium and iron oxides needed in portland cement feed stocks. Portland cement is prepared in a two-step process. Initially, raw materials are blended and then heated to around 3000°F, and fused in a cement kiln to produce a substance called clinker. Next, the clinker and additives are ground to a fine powder to produce portland cement. CCPs may be used as a raw material feed or fly ash may be ground with the clinker. Certain FGD products can also be added into the finished cement as a replacement for natural gypsum.

Portland-Pozzolan Blended Cement

When fly ash is added to cement clinker during or after the grinding process, blended cement is produced. The resulting product, Type IP cement, must conform to ASTM C595 and may contain 15% to 40% fly ash. The composition, properties and behavior of the cement determine the proportions blended.

Aggregates for Concrete Block and Other Precast Concrete Products

Coal fly ash is used in manufacturing concrete block to add plasticity to the concrete mixture and improve the quality of the blocks. Ash addition produces blocks with better texture, better corners and increases mold life. Typically ash is added to replace twenty to thirty percent of the cement. However, at block plants where steam curing is used, ash addition rates may be as high as fifty percent of total cementitious material.

Bottom ash can be used as lightweight aggregate for the production of precast concrete products such as concrete masonry units and other concrete where a low density material is beneficial in reducing weight or loading. The principal use of lightweight aggregates is for block and structural or precast concrete where low unit weight of the end product may be an important factor in the design of the structure. Lightweight aggregate normally has a density around fifty to seventy pounds per cubic foot. These aggregates need to be non-staining and non-reactive because of their use in structural and architectural applications where appearance and durability are important. Conformance to ASTM C330 or ASTM C331 is usually a requirement.

Fly ash lightweight aggregates are commercially produced from firing or chemical bonding processes. One such lightweight aggregate is produced from fly ash and municipal wastewater sludge or paper mill sludge, providing a viable outlet for multiple materials that would otherwise be disposed. Other lightweight aggregates have been produced from high calcium fly ash that has been conditioned, spread and allowed to cure. After curing the material is excavated, crushed, and graded prior to additional curing and use.

Autoclaved Cellular Concrete

This versatile building material currently is produced at 240 plants in forty countries—and it is now being introduced into the USA. When fly ash is utilized, the product, consisting of roughly seventy percent fly ash plus water, cement, lime and aluminum powder, is a porous, lightweight material that offers excellent insulating properties and strength and is resistant to fire, sound, mildew and insects. It can be easily sawed, drilled, screwed and nailed with ordinary carpentry tools. Given the international acceptance this product has received, autoclaved cellular concrete is expected to become a significant outlet for the beneficial use of fly ash in the USA.

Concrete and Asphaltic Pavement Structures

CCPs have been successfully used for decades as a component in both portland cement concrete pavements and asphaltic concrete pavements and through the entire pavement structure from the subbase to the wearing course. The use of CCPs provides a superior performing structure as well as a cost effective measure for state highway departments.

Lime-Fly Ash Base and Subbase

Lime-fly ash (LFA) mixtures are blends of hydrated lime and fly ash mixed with native materials or blended with crushed stone or other aggregates. LFA mixtures have been used as base and subbase beneath flexible asphalt pavements. The mixtures are blended in a central mixing plant or in place, compacted, cured and topped with an asphalt wearing surface. The superior

strength and durability of LFA mixtures, as compared to aggregate alone, allows LFA mixtures to serve as an economic alternative to conventional pavement in many situations.

Cement-Treated Bottom Ash Base and Subbase

Cement treated bottom ash has been used as a substitute for conventional crushed stone or gravel base courses for secondary roads. This product has been especially useful in locations where bottom ash is plentiful and natural aggregates are relatively scarce or expensive.

Concrete Pavements

The principal benefits ascribed to the use of fly ash in concrete are very important for its use in concrete pavements. The benefits include improved workability due to the spherical fly ash particles, reduced water demand, reduced bleeding, increased ultimate strength, reduced permeability, decreased heat of hydration, greater resistance to sulfate attack, greater resistance to alkali-aggregate reactivity, and reduced shrinkage.

Coal fly ash is a key component in the "high performance" concretes that are being developed around the world. In the USA, the Federal Highway Administration (FHWA) is leading the way in high performance concrete technologies, and fly ash is being "rediscovered" in every state.

Asphaltic Concrete Pavements

Asphalt pavement normally consists of a blend of asphalt, coarse aggregate and a fine-grain additive, commonly referred to as a mineral filler. Fly ash has been used since the early 1930s as a mineral filler in asphalt mixes. Many fly ashes have chemical and physical characteristics, particularly low plasticity, which are suitable for use in this application. Specifications normally allow a grain size of seventy to one hundred percent passing a #200 sieve. Often, fly ashes which do not meet specifications for use in concrete will comply with these requirements for use as a mineral filler in asphalt.

Blends of boiler slag and cationic emulsified asphalt have been demonstrated as a practical surface pavement for service road

Block Manufacture

and low volume secondary roads in rural areas. This material has the advantage of low cost and convenience. It can be mixed and stockpiled for later use, even during periods of cold and inclement weather when conventional asphalt may not be available.

Recycled Pavement

Fly ash mixed with lime or portland cement has been used as a binder to recycle secondary road pavements. The pulverized, recycled pavement is combined with the fly ash mixture, compacted to ten inches or more, then covered with a thin asphalt or tar and chip surface. This process offers the benefit of significant cost savings over conventional methods because additional aggregate is not imported to reconstruct the pavement.

Geotechnical Applications

Geotechnical applications for CCPs in projects such as highways, airports, commercial land developments, and public infrastructure systems constitute another major use area for CCPs. In addition to concrete, CCPs have been successfully used in geotechnical projects in several ways including: flowable fill; grouts; roller compacted concrete; structural fill/embankments; road base and subbase; asphalt filler; and soil stabilization

Flowable Fill

Mixtures of CCPs, cement and water have been used as construction backfill in areas where conventional backfilling may be difficult or undesirable. These fluid mixtures flow into areas to be filled and result in a fill with properties equal to, or exceeding traditional backfill materials. A mixture of CCPs, water, sand, and a small amount of cement is typical. In some cases no cement is required.

The savings in using flowable fills results from the reduction in time, equipment and manpower needed and in superior performance, as compared to conventional materials. Flowable fills are especially useful in restricted areas where access for placement and compaction is difficult and where minimal subsequent settlement is desired.

Grouting

Grout is used to strengthen or decrease permeability of structures and subsurface strata by filling voids, and cementing cracks, fissures and other openings. Fly ash adds several useful properties to grout mixes. The fine, uniform particle size, spherical shape and pozzolanic activity of fly ash are all useful qualities.

Grouts containing fly ash have been employed in filling abandoned underground mines to prevent ground subsidence. Ash use in oil well grouting dates back to 1949. In this application, pumpability, reduced bleeding and lower heat of hydration with fly ash grouts are particularly desirable properties. As stated in the section on standards, the American Petroleum Institute has a standard specification for this use of fly ash.

Roller Compacted Concrete

Roller compacted concrete (RCC) is a fill material which is placed using conventional earthmoving equipment such as dump tucks, bulldozers and vibratory compactors. RCC mixes are used for mass concrete in dams, thick pavement bases and similar applications. In such applications earth moving equipment reduces the placement and forming costs that are associated with other concrete construction methods.

RCC mixes have a lower water content and higher ash content than conventional concrete mixes. Fly ash contributes to the strength and cost-effectiveness of the material. The United States Bureau of Reclamation completed the construction of the Upper Stillwater Dam using Roller Compacted Concrete containing large percentages of fly ash. The general contractor completed the project over a five-year period in the 1980s. The dam contains more than one million cubic yards of RCC designed with a compressive strength of 4,000 psi after one year. A total of almost 200,000 tons of low-calcium fly ash was used in the project.

Soil Stabilization

Coal fly ash has been used to supplement or replace portland cement or lime in soil stabilization applications. When ash is used as an ingredient, standardized mix design procedures are available. Design specifications typically include

Stabilized Pavement Base

compaction moisture content, strength and dimensional stability criteria. Procedures for curing, placement and other considerations are typically included. Specifications for fly ash use in soil stabilization have been adopted by several federal government agencies, including the FAA, FHWA, U.S. Army Corps of Engineers, U.S. Bureau of Reclamation, and by numerous state departments of transportation.

Construction Bedding

Bottom ash is widely used as fill to provide support and drainage beneath slabs and small structures, and as pipe bedding. Bottom ash is often the preferred material for these uses because it is easily spread and compacted, is not sensitive to moisture content variations, drains readily and forms a stable base.

Backfill

The qualities that make bottom ash a preferred material for construction bedding also make it desirable as a backfill material for small areas. Bottom ash is uniform, well graded, drains readily, is not sensitive to moisture variations and is relatively light-weight as compared to many natural materials. Bottom ash can be handled, placed and compacted using the same techniques applicable for other natural granular materials.

Structural Fills/Embankments

CCPs are a lightweight, inexpensive material for constructing fills. In this application, CCPs have been used to convert sites with unsuitable topography into valuable, productive property, and for bases and embankments for roadways, parking areas, and building construction. These materials can be placed, spread and compacted using the same equipment applicable for conventional fill materials.

In the United States, documentation for the use of CCPs in structural fills dates back to 1971. Since then, millions of tons have been used in successful land development projects. These sites include housing developments, shopping malls, industrial parks and other types of commercial, residential and industrial developments. Transportation costs and material availability

normally determine if CCPs are a practical alternative to competing native materials. When available in sufficient quantities within competitive haul distances, CCPs have proven to be an excellent borrow material for creating structural fills. The most common material used for structural fills has been low CaO fly ash. High CaO fly ash, bottom ash, FBC ash, stabilized FGD materials, and other types of CCPs have also been successfully used as structural fills.

Many state transportation departments are taking advantage of the beneficial properties and low cost of CCPs to construct roadway embankments. The availability of these inexpensive fill materials eliminates the need for traditional cut-and-fill designs which often involve expensive excavation.

Use of CCPs in highway embankments has been most prevalent in Europe and in urban projects in the United States where borrow materials are limited. Recently, the use of CCPs in high-way embankments and site development has become more prevalent as a result of experience gained through demonstration projects sponsored by CCP producers and highway departments. Increased future use is anticipated due to the success of these projects and the experience and familiarity gained by highway designers and other prospective users. The recent development of ASTM Standard E1861 will also lead to more CCPs being used in structural fill applications.

Manufactured Product Applications

Roofing Granules

A major use of boiler slag is the hard, fine aggregate used in shingles and other roofing products. Several properties of boiler slag make it the preferred material for this use, including natural dark color, hardness, and resistance to ultraviolet radiation. Its glassy composition makes it durable and resistant to oxidation and weathering, thus producing a long lasting surface.

Wallboard

FGD residues from wet lime and limestone scrubbers have been effectively utilized for the production of wallboard for residential and commercial construction. FGD residues from these installa-

Roadway Embankment

Filler in Paint

tions are primarily gypsum $CaSO_4 \cdot 2H_2O$. In order for FGD material to be used in wallboard, several criteria must be satisfied. First, the FGD should contain from 98% to 99% gypsum. Calcium sulfite ($CaSO_3$) is not desirable because in substantial quantities it can change the crystallization and adversely modify the stucco-slurry fed to the wallboard manufacturing line. Water soluble salt components should be limited to prevent delamination of the paper layers from the gypsum core; and fly ash content should be limited to prevent discoloration, adverse crystallization, and improper board forming. Additionally, FGD residues from wet lime scrubbers will require substantial drying before use. FGD residues from other calcium-based scrubber systems typically have high levels of calcium sulfite; and forced oxidation technologies are available to convert them to calcium sulfate.

Filler in Paint, Plastics, and Other Products

Fly ash and in particular cenospheres, have been used in blends of plastics and paints as a mineral filler to enhance mixture properties and to reduce the cost of materials. Cenospheres are hollow fly ash spheres and are often referred to as "floaters" because, with a specific gravity in a range from sixty to eighty percent of that for water, they are naturally buoyant. Clearly, cenospheres can reduce the weight of manufactured products. They also can reduce the cost of some plastic products by reducing the amount of resin that is needed.

The fly ash that is used as a filler may be processed or unprocessed, depending upon the properties needed for a specific product. The major advantage fly ash and cenospheres have over other fillers is their spherical shape, which enables them to fill and flow much more readily than other platy fillers such as clay or calcium carbonate. Also, due to the high temperatures at which CCPs are produced, they are better able to withstand high-temperature manufacturing processes and have been used in a wide range of plastic products for industrial, commercial and domestic purposes.

Fly ash, other than cenospheres, has a specific gravity in a range from 1.8 to 2.8 times that of water. By comparison to cenospheres, a typical fly ash that is used in filler applications will have smaller diameters that fall in a narrow range. Due to their spherical shape, fly ash fillers can withstand extreme pressures. The adhesive, grout, plastic, paint, explosive and automotive industries have all benefited from the use of fly ash as a filler.

Fly ash is used in the manufacture of polyvinyl chloride (PVC) pipe improving productivity factors and lowering raw material cost. Similarly, the durability and strength of vinyl floor coverings are improved with fly ash, the weight of the finished product is decreased, and the raw material costs are reduced.

Cenospheres are utilized in low-density paints for exotic applications, including aircraft carrier deck coatings, and they are used as a filler in automobile undercoatings. In addition to reduced material costs, the crucial properties of improved flowability and very light weight provide specific advantages. Industries that have benefited from the use of cenospheres as a filler include sporting goods, specialty cements, PVC flooring and many others.

Some of the more innovative developments for cenospheres and denser fly ash particles are emerging in the aerospace industry. For example, silver-coated cenospheres are used to fill voids which create radar echoes in the "stealth aircraft". Lightweight composites utilizing CCPs provide the needed weight reduction with no loss in rigidity or strength.

Metallurgical Applications

CCPs are used by the steel industry for many valuable applications. Coal fly ash and bottom ash can be used as insulating cover material to retain heat in ladles of molten steel. These ladle insulators should be flowable and coarse, have a low bulk density and have a wide particle-size distribution. Fly ashes with such characteristics generally are produced by coal-fired stoker boilers.

Most of the newer steel mills in the USA use electric arc furnaces to melt scrap iron and refine it for making specialty products. These furnaces use carbon electrodes charged with an electric current to heat the scrap in a refractory-lined furnace. Both the carbon rods and refractory material are consumed in the process and are very expensive to replace.

To prolong the life of these components, a coarse high-carbon fly ash is injected into the slag, an accumulation of impurities that float at the surface of the molten steel. The combustion of the carbon in the ash generates carbon monoxide and other gasses that "foam" the slag. Foamy slag prolongs the life of the carbon rods and the refractory by insulating the region on the carbon rods and refractory where the surface of the molten steel meets the atmosphere. Additionally, foamy slag promotes the movement of impurities from the molten steel into the slag. Important characteristics for slag foamers are a carbon content greater than fifty percent, a low percentage of fines, a high degree of coarseness, a good particle-size distribution, and a bulk density of greater than forty pounds per cubic foot. Small coal-fired stoker boilers readily produce ash of this quality.

The high melting point and strength characteristics of CCPs make them highly suitable for applications as sintered tiles. Cenospheres as well as denser fly ashes are used to produce insulating refractory compounds for the steel industry.

Composites of aluminum and fly ash have been developed using standard foundry techniques. Additions of solid and hollow particles of fly ash have been successful in reducing the material cost and density of aluminum castings while increasing their performance. Testing of aluminum-fly ash composites shows superior abrasion resistance, increased hardness, higher compressive strength and increased elastic modulus compared to the parent matrix. Composites containing up to fifty-five percent fly ash on a volume basis have been developed. Additionally, cast composites of aluminum and fly ash have been successfully extruded using commercial technology, suggesting even more opportunities for use. The production of fly ash and aluminum composites could make existing foundries more competitive by increasing the market potential for aluminum in applications that traditionally have been dominated by steel. Examples of such markets include both the automotive and the electromechanical machinery industries.

Explosives Manufacturing

Another application for cenospheres is in explosives manufacturing. Cenospheres provide a stable medium for introducing controlled air voids, a requirement for reliable detonation.

Agricultural Applications

Large quantities of CCPs can be utilized for applications in the agricultural industry. The chemical and physical characteristics of CCPs provide many properties that are needed for the production of crops. CCPs are used to replace or augment some of the fertilizers and additives used by farmers today.

Soil Amendment

There are a number of reasons to use CCPs to improve agricultural soils. Most benefits can be categorized as either chemical or physical in nature. Chemical benefits result from supplying essential plant nutrients for growth or by changing the soil pH to make it a more favorable medium for plant growth. Examples of physical changes include increases of water holding capacity when fly ash is added to coarse textured soils and increased water infiltration and soil aggregation due the application of FGD material.

Many CCPs have appreciable levels of elemental calcium and sulfur, nutrients essential to the growth of all plant crops. FGD residue may be pelletized for efficient handling and application onto fields. Crops such as peanuts, potatoes, and evergreens can benefit from the application of FGD residue. The FGD residue is made up primarily of calcium sulfate ($CaSO_4$) and calcium sulfite ($CaSO_3$), which are soluble forms of calcium, and is available in a product which is pH-neutral, (neither acidic nor alkaline). In the case of peanuts, large amounts of available calcium are required by the plant during a certain period of growth known as pegging. If the calcium is not available during this period, the harvest of peanuts will have "pops", or vacant shells, thus severely detracting from the value of the crop.

In cases where CCP storage ponds have been filled to capacity, the establishment of vegetative cover often is a necessary step in converting the pond to an inactive status. Many electric utilities have found that the direct seeding of dewatered storage ponds can be quite effective in the establishment of a vigorous vegetative cover.

Filler in Metal

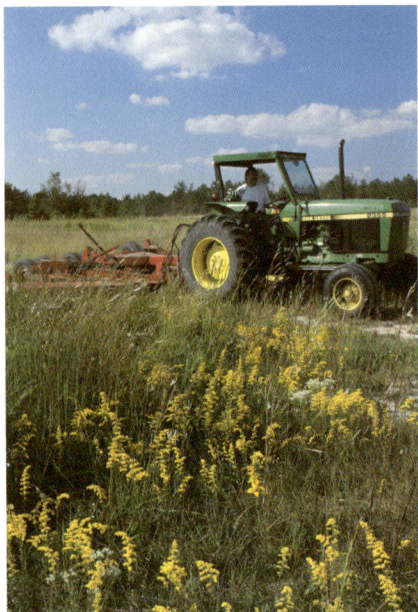

Agricultural Applications

Conversion of Salty Soils

FGD gypsum can be used in the conversion of salty soils to more productive soils. The gypsum is used for exchanging calcium for sodium and removing bicarbonates from soil solution. Several tons of gypsum per acre are usually used. The gypsum must be thoroughly mixed with the soil and not simply plowed under. The treatment must be supplemented by thorough leaching of the soil with irrigation water to leach out some of the sodium sulfate.

Potting and Landscape Soils

Fly ash and FGD residues can be used in the production of potting soil mixtures. When used in this application, CCPs provide air and water holding capacity, nutrients and improve soil texture. These CCPs can be added to peat moss, humus, compost or pine bark mixtures to produce high quality soils.

Soil from Stabilized Sewage Sludge

Dewatered sewage sludge can be combined with high CaO CCPs or a mixture of low CaO CCPs and cement kiln dust, lime, or lime kiln dust to produce a safe and high quality soil. The fine particle size of CCPs and the available alkalinity of the CaO provide the characteristics to dry the sludge, pasteurize the pathogens in the sludge, reduce odor, and provide a granular consistency. The stabilized sludge product has valuable levels of calcium carbonate, nitrogen, organic matter, and other nutrients. The stabilized sludge product has many applications in the agricultural industry as a liming material, soil conditioner, fertilizer, and landscaping soil.

Environmental Applications

The physical and chemical characteristics of many CCPs, along with their availability in dry, conditioned or slurry form, make them very useful for mining and waste management applications.

Coal Refuse and Mine Fires

In several coal mining regions, spontaneous combustion and other causes have created smoldering coal refuse piles and deep mine fires. Fly ash slurry is often used to fill voids and to isolate and cool combustion areas in burning refuse piles. Both ponded ash and conditioned ash have been used in this application to form a slurry which is injected into the fire zone through pipes and boreholes.

For deep mine fires, dry fly ash has been pneumatically injected to directly extinguish burning areas and to create barriers of incombustible material to isolate hot spots.

Mine Subsidence and Acid Mire Drainage Prevention

Large quantities of fly ash have been used to stop or prevent surface subsidence above mined areas. Dry fly ash injected pneumatically, slurried fly ash and fly ash grouts have all been used to fill subsurface voids protecting industrial, commercial, public and residential developments from mine subsidence damage. When alkaline ash is used in these applications a reduction or elimination of acid mine drainage may also result. Alkaline fly ash and mixtures of fly ash and FGD materials have been used successfully in projects to control acid mine drainage from deep mines.

Surface Mine Reclamation

Surface mine areas and mine refuse piles have several characteristics that make reclamation difficult. Adverse properties of these spoil materials that interfere with plant growth include coarse texture and poor water holding capacity, dense compacted surfaces, the presence of acidic materials and the lack of sufficient nutrients. These problems are aggravated when erosion and accelerated surface runoff further prevent the successful establishment of vegetation.

Direct application of fly ash can aid in the successful establishment of vegetation as part of a reclamation program. Addition of fly ash to surface soils improves the physical characteristics of the soil, with the fine material in the fly ash creating a better graded soil texture. This change improves the water holding capacity of the soil and better supports vegetation. Fly ash also provides nutrients and, in the case of alkaline fly ashes, neutralizes acidity. Fly ash typically is added at rates up to four hundred tons per acre to mine spoils as part of revegetation programs.

Landfill Cover

Fly ash and bottom ash are used at municipal waste landfills as daily and intermediate cover and as a component of final cover. The fine grain size of these materials makes them a practical substitute cover material in locations where suitable natural soil materials are unavailable or scarce.

Waste Stabilization

Coal fly ash is an excellent material for use in stabilizing and solidifying biological and industrial sludges and liquid wastes from industrial processes and wastewater treatment. Sludges and liquids from hazardous waste management and site cleanups have also been stabilized using ash. Liquid wastes and sludges are difficult to handle and transport due to their unstable nature. The addition of dry fly ash, alone or in combination with lime kiln dust or portland cement, results in the drying, thickening and stabilization of these materials and improves their handling characteristics. Cementitious reactions that occur upon curing are also a benefit from the use of fly ash as a solidifying and stabilizing agent. These reactions tend to reduce the leachability of metals and other substances that may be contained in the waste. Pozzolans such as fly ash have been recognized by the U.S. EPA as the preferred material for stabilizing certain metal-bearing wastes.

Specialty Applications

Skid Control

One of the major uses of bottom ash and boiler slag is as an agent to prevent skidding on icy roadways in winter. These CCPs are widely used by highway departments for this purpose in regions where inclement winter weather makes driving hazardous. The dark color of bottom ash and boiler slag allows them to absorb radiant energy and aid in the melting process. Bottom ash and boiler slag are superior to sand or crushed stone for this use. The free draining nature of bottom ash and boiler slag reduces freezing and clumping in stockpiles.

Blasting Grit

Processing boiler slag to produce roofing granules also generates graded materials suitable for use as grit in sand blasting. The hard and angular nature of boiler slag, combined with its relatively low cost, makes it an ideal material for use as an abrasive. Additionally, the low free silica content of boiler slag as compared to natural sand is an important health issue.

Marine Applications

Stabilized blocks of fly ash and FGD materials have been used to construct artificial reefs suitable for supporting marine life. Other CCPs, formed into small saucer shaped units, have been used to promote the development of oyster beds. Studies, to date, of marine applications of CCPs have been very encouraging.

Glossary of Terms

The following terms are related to coal combustion product (CCP) production and use.

Agriculture—Use of CCPs as a soil amendment for changing physical and/or chemical characteristics of the soil to improve plant growth.

Aggregate—Lightweight aggregate manufactured from coal fly ash; normal-weight aggregate manufactured from FGD material; and bottom ash or boiler slag.

Backfills—Use of moisture-conditioned fly ash or bottom ash as an alternative to imported borrow for filling trenches, voids behind retaining walls and miscellaneous excavations.

Blasting Grit—Use of boiler slag as substitute for sand or oxide abrasives in cleaning of castings, paint removal, etc.

Boiler Slag—Hard, glassy CCP particles collected from wet-bottom or cyclone furnaces when molten CCP materials flowing from the furnace is quenched in water baths.

Bottom Ash—Solid particles of CCPs which are collected at the bottom of dry-bottom boilers.

Cement and Concrete Products—CCPs used in the manufacture of portland cement, as a raw feed or in a blended cement; and CCPs used as a mixture ingredient in the production of fresh concrete for a variety of uses (See also: Concrete Block; Ready Mixed Concrete, Precast Concrete and Concrete Pipe; and Portland Cement).

Coal Fly Ash Class—Coal fly ash described by the American Society for Testing and Materials in ASTM C 618, Standard Specification for Fly Ash and Raw or Calcined Natural Pozzolan for Use As a Mineral Admixture in Portland Cement Concrete, as Class C or Class F. Also, in common usage, a fly ash may be referred to as a Class C, or high-calcium, fly ash if its lime (CaO) content is greater than about twenty percent by total weight of the fly ash. Similarly, in common usage, fly ash with a lime content less than ten percent by total weight of the fly ash may be referred to as Class F.

Coal Mining Applications—See Mining Industry.

Coal Type—Anthracite, bituminous, subbituminous and lignite.

Concrete Block—Use of fly ash for a portion of the cementitious material, and/or use of bottom ash as a substitute for sand and other fine graded aggregates in the manufacture of building blocks.

Embankments—Use of CCPs as a structural fill above grade for carrying a roadway, parking lot or building, or for gravity dam construction.

Flue Gas Desulfurization Material (FGD)—Lime or powdered limestone combined with oxides of sulfur, collected from the flue gas stream of coal-fired furnaces by means of scrubbers.

FGD Material Solidification—Use of fly ash inter-blended with flue gas desulfurization material to produce a soil-like product that can be compacted and which will gain strength over time.

Filler in Asphalt— (See Mineral Filler in Asphalt).

Filler in Coatings—Use of fly ash as a substitute for various minerals in the manufacture of coatings.

Filler in Metals—Use of fly ash as a substitute for various alloy materials.

Filler in Paints—Use of fly ash as a substitute for titanium dioxide, calcium carbonate, zinc phosphate, etc., in the manufacture of paints.

Filler in Plastics—Use of fly ash as a substitute for glass, ceramics, talc, limestone, and sintered clays in the manufacture of plastics.

Flowable Fill—Use of coal fly ash in a fluid mixture resembling a grout for backfill applications where bearing strengths as well as removability are needed comparable to those of compacted soils. The mixture may have a variety of proportions, with typical ingredients including water and fly ash, along with optional fillers such as bottom ash or sand and small, if any, additions of portland cement (See also: Mining Industry/Underground Grouting; and Oil & Gas Industry).

Geotechnical Applications—Use of CCPs as a replacement for soil fill materials, these applications include flowable fill, grouting, roller compacted concrete, soil stabilization, construction bedding, structural fills and embankments.

Grouting—Use of coal fly ash in a fluid mixture most frequently placed by pumping to underseal, or mudjack, concrete slabs; and to fill hollow-core concrete walls and other building units.

Mineral Filler in Asphalt—Use of fly ash in bituminous concrete mixtures to compensate for deficient fines in the aggregate being used, or to impart other physical characteristics.

Mining Industry—

    Surface Reclamation—Use of CCPs in structural fill applications to restore surface mining areas to original or desirable contours; or to amend mine spoil materials and acid mine drainage.

    Underground Grouting—Use of CCPs as fill material to control surface subsidence conditions, control mine fires, reduce acid mine drainage and sand shifts.

Moisture-Conditioned CCPs—CCPs to which water has been added to control dusting and/or to allow optimum compacted density to be achieved during placement.

Oil & Gas Industry—Use of fly ash with water and appropriate admixtures for grouting and closing wells (See Grouting).

Pavement Bases—Use of fly ash with various activators in pozzolanic stabilized mixtures in the construction of highways, airport runways, parking lots and haul-roads on federal lands.

Portland Cement—Use of fly ash by a cement manufacturer as:

    a raw material feedstock to the kiln in the production of portland cement clinker; or

    an additive to portland cement for the production of blended cements.

Ready Mixed Concrete, Precast Concrete and Concrete Pipe—Use of coal fly ash as a mineral admixture to displace portland cement in varying amounts to improve certain fresh and hardened concrete characteristics, such as workability, strength, permeability and durability.

Reefs—Use of precast fly ash concrete blocks or other shapes and sizes specifically intended for construction of breakwaters or as habitats for fish and/or oysters.

Road Base/Subbase—See: Soil Modification; Soil Stabilization.

Roofing Granules—Use of boiler slag as an inert substitute for fine aggregates, or use of fly ash as an asphalt filler.

Scrubber Material—See Flue Gas Desulfurization Material.

Snow and Ice Control—Use of bottom ash or other CCPs as an alternative to sand for road de-icing operations and skid control.

Soil Amendment—See Agriculture.

Soil Modification—Any change to in-place soils that results in immediate effects that can expedite highway pavement construction operations. These changes can be measured in terms of moisture reduction, improved California Bearing Ratio (CBR) and/or decrease in plasticity.

Soil Stabilization—A permanent change to in-place soils that makes significant improvements in the soil mixture characteristics and allows the soil layer to be assigned a structural support value as an integral part of a pavement structure.

Structural Fills—Use of CCPs in an embankment application to improve the topography and/or provide foundation support for commercial, residential or other construction.

Wallboard—Use of FGD material having a satisfactory gypsum (calcium sulfate) content in the manufacture of building panels.

Waste Solidification and Stabilization—Use of coal fly ash or CCPs either alone or inter-blended with lime and/or portland cement or other agents to encapsulate or immobilize municipal sludges, non-toxic and toxic materials, and non-hazardous and hazardous materials (See also: FGD Material Solidification).

Selected References

The following brief list of publications was selected from ACAA's library of available titles. These documents provide fundamental information concerning the management and use of CCPs. ACAA's web site may be visited to obtain other resources and to review a more comprehensive publication list. Additional information may be obtained by contacting ACAA.

- *Production and Use of Coal Combustion Products (CCPs)—* Annual Reports
- *Management & Use of CCPs*—International Symposium Proceedings
- *Management & Use of CCPs*—Educational Program for Managers
- *Ash At Work*—Newsletter
- *Fly Ash Facts for Highway Engineers* (FHWA)
- *State Regulations Governing the Use of Coal Combustion Products*
- *Increased Fly Ash Use Under the Climate Challenge Program*
- Technical and Environmental Fact Sheets, Guides and Standards (ASTM and EPA)
- Videos, Slides and Promotional Materials
- *Publication List*
- *Membership List*
- Internet Site—http://www.ACAA-USA.org

United States Capitol Building

Construction of fly ash concrete building continues in cold weather conditions.

Subjects